ONSIGNOR WILLIAM BARRY MEMORIAL LIBRARY
BARRY UNIVERSITY
27 .S8
wart, George Rippey, 1 010101 000
: an autobiography / Georg
0 2210 0027871 5

D1001032

GN
27
.S8

156680

Msgr. Wm. Barry Memorial Library
Barry College
Miami, Fl. 33161

STEWART

MAN AN AUTO...

MAN: an Autobiography

OTHER BOOKS BY GEORGE R. STEWART

BRET HARTE

ORDEAL BY HUNGER · JOHN PHOENIX

EAST OF THE GIANTS · DOCTOR'S ORAL

STORM · NAMES ON THE LAND

GEORGE R. STEWART

MAN

AN AUTOBIOGRAPHY

HOMO SUM...

RANDOM HOUSE · NEW YORK

Barry University Library
Miami, FL 33161

FIRST PRINTING

Copyright, 1946, by George R. Stewart

Published simultaneously in Canada by
Random House of Canada Limited

Manufactured in the United States of America
Designer: Ernst Reichl

GN
27
.S8

156680

To Canis, my oldest friend

Contents

MAN: an Autobiography

1

I explain my intentions

I, Man, having attained some maturity of years, feel a desire to write my autobiography. Almost everyone who does so, I remember, states at the beginning just why he is thus making an exhibition of himself—either his grandchildren urged him, or he wanted to justify himself to the world, or something else. I, who am nothing if not conventional, shall do the same.

My explanation, then, is this. I, Man, am thoroughly tired of the various so-called histories of me. First, they are badly proportioned, giving up nearly all their space to the last three thousand years, although what I have done during that time is not nearly so notable as what I did earlier. Second, they make a tedious and complicated matter out of what is really a simple one.

My life-story, as thus told, becomes an immense piling-up of gossipy detail. (I mean such matters as the rise and fall of empires.) The gossip may be interesting enough, but it means little. And by its massing into chapters and volumes it produces a final effect of complication and uncertainty—and, too often, of boredom.

If I may attempt an epigram (and that, I am afraid, is one of my weaknesses), I should say that in most histories, "You cannot see Man because of men."

I understand that any individual may wish to know, and should know, many details about his own country, province, and town—or even about his own street. But he cannot wish to know equally about all the other countries, provinces, and so forth, and he cannot possibly be able to know so much about them, even if he wishes. Individuals of all countries, however, should know about Man.

As every writer of an autobiography may be expected to do, I shall doubtless make some mistakes and misjudgments about myself. Being a rather stupid and lazy fellow, I do not read as many thick books as I should. I have realized also for a long time that I am not wholly accurate by nature. Besides, since this is my own story, I shall now and then make free to write a little in the manner of a poet, broadly, striking at the main idea, and trying to make the reader feel as well as understand. I may not therefore put in every *perhaps* and *probably* and every *either . . . or*, but I shall try always to tell truly the main story.

There will, of course, be more uncertainties in the earlier part than in the later. Anyone telling the story of his own first years has to work from some not-too-trustworthy family stories, a few colorless records of birth and death, and his own childish recollections, with which he probably mingles unknowingly some fairy-tales his nurse told him. Or, when written records fail, he may use the evidence of great-grandfather's sword and pewter mug, and other odds and ends of heirlooms which have survived fires and migrations. In my earlier years I also have to use such scraps and bits, chiefly of stone.

Fortunately, as I have said, my history is really simple, and I hope to express its essentials in one volume of moderate size. Condensing so strictly, I may sometimes leave out matters which seem important to some people. But I shall do the best I can.

In one way at least, my task is made easier than that of the historians. I, Man, am writing about Man. My interest therefore is in what happened to me and of what I did, and so I am not much concerned as to which of my races, or tribes, or individuals accomplished this or that. I hope not to confuse the essential "What was done?" behind the less important "Who did it?"

Having considered all these difficulties, I still think that my life has followed simple lines, and (thus far) is as plain as an old-fashioned novel. Let me, then, begin at the beginning, and come on down through time.

2

The family tree

Autobiographies, I note again, offer in an early chapter some information about ancestry, for example, "The first of our line, a certain William de Villebec, came over with the Conqueror." There is the statement about family connections also, "I thus find myself related, though distantly, with the Scurrisons of Maryland, and probably with those of Derbyshire as well."

I, Man, can trace *my* ancestry clear back to an ancient fish, and thus I definitely claim family connections with all animals having backbones. I pass quickly over these older ancestors, however, not indeed because I am ashamed of their low social standing, or otherwise. But what I have inherited from them has come to be more a part of my world than of myself. Just as I must accept night and day, so I must accept having lungs that breathe air, and blood of about the same saltiness as sea-water.

Coming down much closer, I arrive at an ancestor known as Primitive Mammal, a kind of great-great-grandfather. Not only did I descend from him, but also all the other mammals, such as horses, dogs, whales, bats, and hippopotami. A little curiously, however, although I always consider myself to be more advanced than any of these others, I have in many ways changed less from Primitive Mammal than they have. For he was something of a jack-of-all-trades, being able to run, climb, swim, eat many foods, and get along under varying conditions. Most of the other mammals, as they developed, took up specialties, such as fast running, or cud-chewing, or gnawing, or eating only meat; but I kept on being jack-of-all-trades —and, for a long time at least, master-of-none.

Primitive Mammal was a tree-climber, and my later ancestors, who were his descendants, lived in trees through what people like to call "countless centuries." This long period of jumping and swinging among the branches left a tremendous imprint upon the make-up and habits of all the descendants, including me. Sometimes I think I can understand myself best by considering that I am merely a tree-dweller recently come down to live on the ground. Yes, even now when I have fully become Man, I am shaped in body and confirmed in habits because of that ancient way of life.

First of all, look at my hand. It is something I am enormously proud of. Yet it was originally nothing more than a gadget to keep me from falling out of the tree. All tree-animals have to develop something of the kind. Sharp claws are enough for small animals, and with them a tree-toad can climb right up and down the bark. Larger animals may develop a kind of hook, as the sloth has done; but more of them, like the apes and monkeys, go in for grasping. Thus, in spite of my being so proud of it, my hand is by no means one of my most distinctive possessions.

Again, tree-animals were bound to be as much concerned with *up* and *down* as with *forward*, *back*, and *sideways*; and every time they climbed, they took the upright position. So they easily came to sit or stand upright. This is true, you will notice, not only of the apes and monkeys, but also even of such climbers as squirrels and bears. Thus my upright position goes back to the trees.

Still again, there are my food habits. If an animal eats leaves or twigs, he can have an unlimited supply of one kind of food in the trees. But leaves and twigs are low-grade stuff, and so a larger animal living on them will have to eat a great deal and have a big digestive system. This, however, means having a large paunch, which is not a convenient thing to swing about from branch to branch. So it was natural for my ancestors to eat a little of everything, including some leaves and twigs. Also, they could not commonly find enough to eat at one place and time, but foraged around, eating at one spot, and a few hours later filling up again somewhere else. They did not, like the dog, make a kill, eat heavily, and then go easily without eating for a full day. Thus in harmony with that ancient living in the trees is my present ability to eat almost anything, and my habit of eating three or more times a day.

Take also the matter of senses. Touch seems to be the most primitive, and exists even with creatures who have no eyes and ears. With me, touch still remains as the basic sense, and actual contact is necessary for the fullest expression of love itself. My ancestors depended also largely upon smell, which is tied up with taste and very valuable for locating and distinguishing food. But as life went on, a question seems to have developed as to the ranking of smell, sight, and hearing. Again, for my ancestors, their living in trees supplied the answer. Except for a very small animal, smell was not much good away from the ground. Even though a trail of scent might lie along one branch, it did not jump the break from one branch or tree to another. Sound, however, was as reliable in the trees as on the ground, and sight was even somewhat better, because tree-animals were not hidden in jungle or tall grass. Of the three, sight was also the most important for tree-animals, for it was the only one which enabled them to leap accurately from branch to branch. So my rating of senses—smell the least, hearing in the middle, sight the greatest—is proper for good living in the trees. Even the ability to use two eyes as one, a most distinctive trait of mine, may also somehow be tied up with this importance of accuracy in judging distance for jumps.

From reliance upon sight follows naturally the habit of daytime living. My ancestors became rather pitifully dependent upon light. I, Man, followed after them in this also.

Less certainly, the change from snout to face went along with my dependence on sight and so with life in the trees. As long as my ancestors had a good sense of smell, they naturally stuck their snouts right up to whatever snail or berry they were about to eat, and with eyes a couple of inches back of nostrils they could look as well as sniff. Once they depended on sight, they investigated with the fore-paws, and adjusted the thing to the proper distance for best sight. After that, the snout was of less use.

Besides the nostrils, the snout housed the jaw and teeth. But a big slashing fighting jaw is not much use unless you have solid ground underfoot. Imagine, for comparison, a couple of heavyweights boxing upon a stretched net such as you see beneath a flying-trapeze in the circus. Neither could probably ever land a heavy enough blow to knock the other out, for the simple reason that whenever he started to swing, his footing would give way. In trees also there was generally no sure footing, and so a powerful jaw was of less use. Although this lack of use for snout and jaw would not actually make them disappear, there would at least be thenceforth less reason why they should *not* disappear.

Closely tied up with the jaw also went my greatest pride, that is, my brain. A powerful jaw demanded powerful muscles to work it, and some of them ran up along the temples and the sides of the skull above them. I still have remnants of these muscles, and by putting a finger to your temple you can feel them every time you chew. (You can even see them working, especially if there is no hair, and so has arisen the saying that when a bald-headed person eats, you can see his brains work.) Anyway, when these muscles were powerful, as they were in my earlier ancestors, they took up a large part of the front of the head, and there was not so much room for the brain. This shows up strikingly even in the gorilla, who has a tremendous jaw and jaw-muscles (and compressed brain) even though he is very man-like in other ways. (But the gorilla lives mainly on the ground, and may have developed his jaw to some extent after he came out of the trees.)

Whether brain grew because jaw-muscles shrank, or whether jaw-muscles shrank because brain grew, or whether both resulted from something else—all of that involves the whole problem of cause and effect, and is something over which I, Man, being a stupid fellow, always get confused. (I hope to find a place to take up that whole problem later.) Just for the present, I shall merely let it go for what I know surely: that is, the brain got larger *and* the jaw-muscles got smaller.

Nevertheless, living in trees certainly made mere power less important than quickness, agility, skill, and cunning.

All these matters which I have been discussing are very important and fundamental. Some others are not so important, and their connection with the trees is more doubtful, but still I think them interesting.

Throwing with aim, that is, actually to hit something and not just to express rage, is one of my special traits, and a very useful one. Scarcely any other creature does it, although—as you can see in any zoo—monkeys and even bears can catch. Throwing seems to be connected with trees, for the simple reason that anything loosed from a tree will fall. So you can notice that many tree-animals, even squirrels, will drop bits of bark or other things upon animals beneath the tree. This dropping is embarrassing, or alarming, to the one on the ground, and it is pleasant to the one in the tree. Of course this vague dropping or tossing is very different from real throwing. Still, it seems the beginning.

My usual disregard for sanitation and cleanliness may also go back to the trees. From the branches everything dropped to the ground and was gone. There was a kind of natural garbage- and sewage-disposal. On the other hand, animals like wolves had to learn to keep their dens moderately clean and decent. (This is one reason, I suppose, why it is easier to house-break a puppy than a baby.) Also, large forests existed only in rainy countries, and my ancestor was kept more or less clean by the rain. At the same time he had no easy way of getting any other water for bathing. At first perhaps he may have licked himself like a cat, but as his snout receded, he probably lost such a habit. So from living in trees may have come my native carelessness in such matters, which seems to be overcome only at a high stage of civilization.

Finally, most of the real tree-dwellers live in tropical forests, because a northern woodland of pine fails to supply much food, and one of oak and maple has the disconcerting habit of losing its leaves in winter. Much about me also points back to an origin in the tropical region or near it. To begin with, my nearest relatives still live exclusively in the tropics. Although in many ways I thrive best in a cooler climate, I still seem to resent boisterous weather—especially cold winds. I quite naturally say "cold and miserable." A tree-animal in a temperate forest can get through the leafless and lifeless winter only by sleeping through the worst season or by storing food, but I am unable to hibernate, and have no natural habit of storing food. This last is something like sanitation, in that I have to learn it as I develop toward civilization.

My ancestors lived so long in the trees and became so well adapted to tree-life that they even developed the habit of swinging by the hands from branch to branch as an ordinary means of moving about. Along with his habit some changes developed in the shape of certain bones, and those bone-shapes still persist in my skeleton, although they are no longer of much use to me. Nevertheless, I have often noticed how naturally children swing from ring to ring on their playground apparatus, and how much they enjoy doing it.

3

How they came down from it

My ancestors thus became excellently fitted for life among the branches, but nevertheless they could scarcely have lived there all the time. In a few places perhaps rain came so regularly that even a good-sized animal could get enough water by lapping it from leaves, branches, and his own hair. But in most places there were dry seasons, and during them the larger tree-dwellers had to come down to some pool or stream. Once on the ground, they doubtless scurried about a little for the fun and novelty of it (especially the adventurous young), and at the same time they found certain kinds of food.

All this brings me to a decisive point in my story—the descent from the trees to the ground. There are complicated theories to explain this shift, but like so much else in the story, it can be kept simple enough. After all, it was merely a kind of migration, and the most ordinary cause of migration is too many people. My ancestors were presumably what are known as "successful animals," that is, they were well adapted to their way of life, and were constantly increasing in numbers. Therefore they were constantly spreading farther and farther throughout whatever forest-area they inhabited. Eventually, after an indefinite number of thousands of years, they necessarily came to the edge of the forest—but still the increase in numbers continued. A forest, then as now, did not end along a sharp line. More likely, there was a transition-belt of many miles where bits of excellent woodland mingled with scrubbier growth, and that in turn began to give place to larger and larger savannas of grassland. In such a country my ancestors would spend more and more time on the ground, returning to the trees at night.

Once they had made the adjustment to the half-and-half way of life, pressure of population would begin again, and those along the edge were inevitably pushed out farther into the brush country. Since these individuals spent most of their active life on the ground, they gradually lost some of their knack of swinging from branch to branch, and their descendants no longer felt at home in the trees during the day.

At last the inevitable happened again. (There must always be a first time.) Some band wandered too far, or stayed too long at some favorite foraging ground, or delayed because one of them had run a thorn into his foot. As twilight gathered, they faced—first of their race—the necessity of spending a night on the ground. Whimpering in fright, not even aware of just what had happened, they followed habit by scrambling to the top of a rock or by creeping into some thicket, even though the bushes were not big enough for climbing. They whimpered again as the last light faded. Perhaps a night-ranging wolf-pack found them; perhaps they were lucky.

Certainly, however, what had happened once would happen again—and always more frequently, as familiarity with the ground and pressure from behind led the bands to wander farther. By forced experience, much was learned, no matter how slowly: that a tiger could no more climb certain rocky cliffs than he could climb a tree, or that a low thorn-bush might baffle a lion. Even if the marauder took a toll, that was only to be expected; the leopard had preyed upon them in the trees also. At least we know for certain that in the end they left the trees, even for sleeping.

There is also the idea of climatic change to explain the great migration—that as the centuries grew colder or drier, the forest thinned out and eventually disappeared. According to that idea, the number of creatures remained the same while the number of trees decreased. But this is only getting at the problem of over-population in a more complicated manner. In any case, the two explanations differ only in the more distant causes, and the process would have been the same, either way.

At this point Ape-Man (or whatever you wish to call him) took a road different from those of the gorilla and the chimpanzee. Those two stuck, so to speak, halfway between the trees and the ground. They still live partly on the ground and partly in the trees, and are not as thoroughly at home in the trees as the gibbon is, or as thoroughly at home on the ground as I am.

This descent from the trees, even though it occurred gradually over a period of many centuries, was nevertheless a time of supreme crisis. The stupendous question, upon which all the rest of the story was to hang, was simply this: were these creatures going to fall back upon all-fours, or were they going to continue their tree-dwelling habit of walking on two legs?

With most great crises I find difficulty in imagining that what happened was not the only thing which could have happened. With this one, however, there is a fine object-lesson in the baboon.

The baboon also came down to the ground after a long period in the trees. He kept some of his old traits—a good hand, wide range of food, reliance on sight and hearing, daylight habits. According to some stories, he has even kept and developed the habit of throwing with aim. But, though he still sits upright, he dropped back to his four feet for walking. Thus he took the road of ground-dwelling animals, and became very much like a dog. He has the great fighting jaw and teeth, and the rather cramped brain which goes with them. Also, since he uses his front paws for walking, he cannot really use them as hands. Because he thus went through the same crisis of a descent from the trees to the ground, the baboon has some interesting traits in common with me, although he is not nearly so close to me in blood as are some others.

My ancestors, however, came to depend more and more on their hind legs for walking, and thus kept their hands free to be hands. Of course they did not choose this way consciously because it led toward the future. All I can say is that by that time they had apparently lost the habit of using their hands for walking.

I have presented a whole list of traits which sprang from having lived in trees. Anyone might think that there would be a much longer list of important traits which developed from living on the ground. But that is not so. Thus, as I said before, I really ought to think of myself as a tree-animal who came to the ground on the day before yesterday, and am still living there with only one important change to my body.

That one is the foot. It is really my most distinctive possession, even though I do not boast about it, as I do about my hand. It is also one of my most valuable possessions. There are tremendous advantages in being able to move about and at the same time use the hands for carrying things or for other purposes. Without this ability the story would be so vastly different that it would hardly be the same story at all. By developing a foot which I used for walking and running and for very little else, I escaped being left in the box the gorilla is in. He has neither very good hands nor very good feet, but four of something in between—and so he does not have the best advantages of either.

Still, the foot is one of my weakest parts. Even yet it seems hardly big enough and strong enough for the work it has to do, so that again I seem to be a creature who has just come down from swinging between branches. My foot is easily hurt or broken. Such a two-legged creature as the ostrich seems to have a much tougher foot for running on rough ground. Also the ostrich can kick. But any person who kicks with an uncovered foot hurts himself more than the other fellow—and so I am not by nature a kicker. I would probably be much better off with an ostrich-foot, or even with a cloven hoof like Satan, who was thus, I suppose, equipped for continually walking up and down upon the earth, as was anciently reputed to be necessary in his line of work.

Now that I have mentioned him, I am reminded of the saying:

> *Satan finds some mischief still*
> *For idle hands to do.*

Such a proverb, like a good many others, amuses me because of its complete misunderstanding of what has really happened in the story. When those ancestors came down from the trees, they no longer had to hold on to branches, and yet they did not use their hands for standing or walking. This left their hands idle, and they could use them constantly for all sorts of things—some mischievous, but many others highly useful, and some daringly experimental. In fact these idle hands gradually changed everything and worked out civilization—which may or may not be at the Devil's prompting, according to how you feel about it!

In any case, the relation of hand and foot is interesting. The foot is like a self-sacrificing person who subordinates himself for the good of the whole enterprise, and gets no thanks or honor for it—a sort of first unsung hero. Yet my foot is something unique in nature, whereas my hand is only somewhat better than that of an ape or monkey. When anyone thinks of hands as enabling him to use tools, he forgets that, except by walking on his feet, he would be unable to move a tool from place to place, unless he carried it in his mouth.

My essential foot must have developed slowly during that long period of leaving the trees and living more and more on the ground. People are likely to consider such a time as involving great hardships, thinking that the migrating creature would be at a disadvantage in unfamiliar surroundings. Actually it may be the other way round. Certain abilities which are only ordinary in an old way of life may give almost miraculous advantages in a new one. For instance, living on the ground was largely adjusted to the sense of smell, and my ancestors were almost unique in depending on sight. Thus they had the advantage of a secret weapon over the other ground animals.

Again, the great killers of the ground ranged mostly at night. Because my ancestors were adjusted to tree-life, they ranged during the day, and so had very little chance of running foul of a tiger. At night they could get into some cranny, and be moderately secure. Perhaps they were even more secure, for in trees the leopard was used to hunting them, as he still hunts the monkeys; but on ground the lion and the tiger had long-established habits of hunting other kinds of prey. Thus these newcomers to the ground, like the rabbits in Australia and many other transplanted animals, may have left their old enemies behind and not have found new ones.

Their very knowing about trees helped tremendously with this safety, as it has ever since. Most ground-animals could not climb, and as long as one of my ancestors was within jumping distance of a tree, he could be confident, even impudent. Doubtless many a time he teased a buffalo until the last moment, and then swung to a branch, enjoying the frustration of the charging monster.

On the whole, I cannot see just where the shift from trees to ground was very precarious. Already my ancestors were fairly large, possibly even larger than I am. But even if one of them stood no more than four feet tall, still there was no chance of his being snapped up by a fox or weasel. On the open plain he did not need to keep an eye cocked skyward against a swooping hawk or eagle. When crossing the grassland, to be sure, he gave room to the bison-bull and the stallion, but they did not try to prey upon him. When he foraged in the river-shallow, he came to know the terror of that floating log which suddenly became a crocodile. At night the lion, the tiger, and the leopard were real terrors. With the wolf, however, he was probably on even terms, and if the wolf ran in a pack, so too did he.

Yes, from the beginning, I should say, these new migrants from the trees foraged and lived in bands. There is indeed one theory about the "old man" who with a few wives and an assorted lot of children ranged about, and drove off his own sons as soon as they became rivals. But all actual peoples of whom there is record have lived in bands or tribes, and so I think that even before I was Man my ancestors followed the model of the baboon more than that of the gorilla.

Such a band lived, on the ground as formerly in the trees, by foraging about and eating food wherever it was to be found. There were birds' eggs and nestlings hidden in the grass, as there had been among the leaves—and it was still possible to climb back into a tree after a nest which was seen from below. Besides fruit, nuts, and buds, in the open grassland there was a new and rich supply of food in the ripe seeds of grasses. Certainly this newcomer to the ground, slow of foot and weak of jaw, did not suddenly become a mighty hunter. He was not an attacker, or beast of prey, except for snails and grubs and young birds, which he picked up almost as if they were fruit or eggs. He let the rabbit bound away without thinking that he might pursue it. As for the deer and bison, they were almost creatures of another world. Perhaps after centuries he learned, like the bear, to turn over a rotten log and pounce upon the flustered wood-rat scurrying from beneath. But on the whole, a creature who had eaten a little of almost everything in the trees went on eating a little of almost everything on the ground.

The band moved slowly, foraging as it went. Around the edges, I should think, the more active and bolder males ranged more widely. Toward the center fed the mothers and the scuttling young ones. Since everyone still walked with a stoop, a baby rode easily upon the mother's back and shoulders, twining little arms and fingers into the long head-hair.

If danger threatened, the mothers and young moved off first, and the fathers covered the rear, roaring out defiance. By daylight they might (like the baboons) even stand off a leopard. Weakness would come with the twilight, but before darkness the band drew off to some rocky cliff or high place. Then came the nothingness of sleep, and a fresh day afterwards.

Thus, for defense, I think that they were well enough equipped. If one band sighted another, the males on each side perhaps reared up to look curiously, roared from a distance, and sheered off. Unless it were time of famine and they clashed over some feeding-ground, they had no reason for fighting, and they lacked the hunter instinct to make them wish to fight without reason.

Although the band as a whole could defend itself, whatever killer hung on the flanks cut off the failing old and the foolish young, and all those who fell behind by disease or accident. Night too might bring its terror even for the strongest, and the half-human scream rose suddenly, and was cut off short, as the killer sprang. But the band as a whole only became the more vigorous because its weaker members were the quickest to be cut off.

As for the individuals themselves, all of them differed a little from the individuals of another band living under different conditions in another kind of country. But within one band, they were all remarkably alike, except for sex and age. Life as they lived it allowed little chance to be individual. A tendency to grow fat was as good as a death-warrant. If one of them became near-sighted and could not find much food, he grew weak, lingered behind, and soon screamed for his last time. If one of them developed illusions of grandeur and thought he could kill the lion single-handed, he soon had his chance. But those who in some way rose above the average also ran the risk of their greatness. The bold and strong one who sprang to the front fell before the leopard's rush, and the prudent and average hangers-back scattered to safety. The investigator who ate the new berry and died because it was poisonous might be classed as an early martyr to science —but he was dead! Thus the law of tooth and nail, more rigorous than taboo or social censure, frowned upon any such luxury as going your own way.

For these same reasons, this was the supreme era for

all-round education; there was no practicing a specialty. Even leadership was not much needed, for a foraging band drifted hither and thither as those on the edges found better feeding in one direction or another. When all were so much alike, all desired the same thing, and there was little chance for clash of individual wills as to what the band should or should not do.

Even so, there were probably many fights, especially among the males, about food and mates and other personal matters. My ancestors were neither thoroughgoing and solitary individualists like the cats, nor were they contented herd-animals like the sheep. They were probably more like the baboons, who live in a band but are notorious for their squabblings. This tradition of social disturbances and discontent has been my heritage ever since.

Thus, in one way or another, the bands survived. The one great crisis of the shift from tree to ground was not defense or food, but the question of dropping back upon all fours. If that had happened, the four hands of the tree-animal would have had to become four hand-like feet, and even the best brain would have had no means by which to express itself. Thus the road would have led toward a gorilla or super-baboon, not toward a creature with two good hands and two good feet, able to make use of all the advantages of that combination.

4

I become I

DURING all this time a great deal of water would have flowed under the bridges, if there had been any bridges. As far as the period of living in the trees is concerned, no one can do much better than to say that it was many thousands of centuries. The period of getting adapted to the ground, with the development of the foot and other things, has been estimated at six million years. That is a great deal more time than has elapsed since, because by its end we are down to the comparatively recent date of about 1,000,000 B. C.

So, if I have given any idea that my ancestor descended and suddenly developed his feet, I hope that I have now corrected that impression. In the same ample time, other changes occurred, although most of them are details into which I do not need to go. Perhaps even a million years ago the hair began to disappear, a very mysterious matter. Most changes involve some obvious advantage, but the loss of hair seems a disadvantage, especially since the result was to leave it with a tendency to grow troublesomely long on the head and face. Obviously the hair must have been lost at some time and place when the climate was warm, but that stops far short of explaining things. About the long hair on the head, I have my own theory that it may remain because the baby used to cling to the mother's back, as they do still with monkeys. Long hair would have been useful for the baby to get a grip in, and anything having to do with the raising of babies is the less likely to disappear.

Much more important than the loss of hair, was the continued change of the head. The snout kept shrinking back; the teeth, jaw, and jaw-muscles grew smaller. At the same time, the brain grew larger and more skillful.

I, Man, at this point have thus arrived at a somewhat ticklish place in my story, one at which the likeness to an ordinary autobiography breaks down a little. So far I have been referring to "my ancestors," because I feel myself something essentially different from that ape-like contraption which came down from the trees. But in that case, just when did I, Man, first begin to be? Some scientists might answer that the question has no real meaning, because I did not begin at some particular time, as an individual is conceived or born. Others seem to think that I was Man as soon as I had my proper feet. I myself am a common-sense sort of fellow, and cannot see the matter in either of those ways. I think that the question has a meaning, and also I insist that being Man means more than having a particular kind of foot, and more even than the whole bodily development. If, for instance, there should be discovered a civilized people exactly like me except for having ostrich-feet, I think that I would have difficulty in denying them. On the other hand, if there should be a race with the proper feet but otherwise living like gorillas, I doubt whether I would accept them.

Moreover, such discoveries as the Pekin man have put the whole matter on a new basis. Here is one whom scientists do not even admit as a member of the same genus, much less of the same species—that is, on the shape of his bones, he is not even Homo, but is classified as Sinanthropus or Pithecanthropus. Yet he had all the beginnings of the way of life which I consider human. He made and used tools, he used fire, he apparently cooked his meat, he probably had language. Anyone doing all those things deserves, in my opinion, to be called Man, no matter what kind of feet he walked on, or what the exact shape of his skull.

The startling fact about the Pekin man is this: that even with a body which was still rather ape-like, he had a good enough brain to develop the basic human ways and means of life.

From this point on, therefore, I shall drop all talk of ancestors, and consider that I, Man, have been born.

5

I get tools and speech

I, MAN, still live a life which rests firmly upon what I might call "the essential five." Of these, the Pekin man apparently had four, and possibly even the fifth. Since they thus existed with a creature who physically must be classed as Ape-man, I doubt whether anything that can really be called Man was ever without them. These five are—tools, speech, fire, cookery, and clothing. Tools and speech developed first.

The use of tools came to me, I think, very easily and naturally. To begin with, it may have arisen by what can be called a lucky accident of history. In the trees I had grown accustomed to gripping a branch, and even to this day my relaxed hand contracts to a half-grasping shape. When I first came to the ground and walked on two legs, I must actually have felt more comfortable if my strangely empty hands had something to grip on. (Even yet, millions of people habitually walk holding a handbag or cane.) The most natural thing to carry about at first, now that I no longer needed always to grasp a real branch, would be a dead one which I picked up from the ground.

Having such a stick in my hand, I actually had a tool, even if I did not know it. Eventually, however, it would come in handy for knocking down fruit and nuts, and what began as a mere carry-over habit was confirmed as being useful. Then in panic at being suddenly attacked, I might strike without letting go of the stick—and it had become a club!

From the beginning, the fathers probably took more readily to tools than the mothers, whose hands were too often busy caring for their babies. But the fathers with their idle hands could come more easily to carry sticks and stones and to use them more and more skillfully. So it has been ever since, and a proper mother is still likely to confuse a chisel and a screw-driver.

As for the making of tools, I do not think that there is as much distinction between using and making as some people have thought. The very picking up of a stick is in a way the manufacture of a tool, and the breaking of a dead branch from a tree is even more so. Besides, even from my beginnings on the ground, I had more tools available than I knew what to do with.

The most obvious ones were my old friends the branches, but on the ground I soon became familiar with bones also. Ranging about, I often scared the vultures from picking the carcass of some bison or stag. As I looked, what was really a whole potential tool-shop lay before me—thigh-bones ready-made for clubs, horns or antlers for awls, shoulder-blades for scrapers. Only my inexperience and lack of need held me back. I could not use a scraper if I had nothing to scrape and no idea about scraping.

Also I learned about stones. They were somewhat like bones, but very different from sticks. After a while (a few million years or so, that is) I must have begun to like stones and carry them around as if they were sticks. They had the special uses which go with chunkiness, weight, and hardness, instead of length and lightness. They were useful for throwing. They were good for all kinds of pounding, especially for cracking nuts; I needed some such device, now that my teeth and jaws were weaker. Perhaps by now also I had learned the lesson, a difficult one for a former tree-animal, that tasty roots and tubers were to be had by digging into the ground. Certain stones were handy for such digging.

Then it happened sometimes, when I was digging or pounding, the stone struck against another and broke in two. Suddenly, where before I had had only a rounded stone, there was a new and different sharp-edged thing which might cut the hand—something to wonder at and play with, and to use.

Thus in a world overrun with sticks, stones, and bones, many tools were available, naturally or by accident. What held me back was not my inability to make, but my inability to use. Yet the tools lay ready at hand, once the mind fit to use them should develop.

In this mental development nothing helped more than my using of language. Not only did language enable my individuals to share ideas, but also it stimulated their thinking and helped them actually to attain and classify knowledge.

A certain detail in the shape of the skull is good evidence that the Pekin man, and even the more primitive Java man, had developed sufficiently to be able to talk enough for his purposes. As one of my modern philosophers has put it, he could tell you that the evenings were drawing in, and his feet hurt.

Naturally, language did not start all at once. Most animals obviously can communicate in some degree by sounds. Gesture also can be very eloquent indeed, as when a skunk raises his tail.

My language, however, goes much further, and no one is sure just how it developed. In fact, its origin is one of those delightful subjects in which one theory is still as good as another. So I might as well rush in with the one I prefer.

Language, I think, may well have sprung from two sources, of which the one produced the verb and the other the noun. I, more than many animals, was full of grunts, groans, howls, and snorts, and there was little restraint on my giving vent to them. I was not required, like the cow, to spend long hours in silent cud-chewing; or, like the panther, to range the forest in soft-footed stealth; or, like the rabbit, to nibble silently for fear of being pounced on. Most of my noises expressed in some manner the way I was feeling at the moment. Therefore, each yelp or squeal or burble was really a vague sentence beginning with the words, "I feel . . ." Some half-formed cry like "Ouch!" might be translated, "I feel sudden pain!" After a while, when a creature had as good a brain as mine, the sounds would be more standardized, and their meanings fitted to the situation. Thus "Ouch!" might be used playfully, when the individual felt no real pain, or it might warn a child not to pick up a bee.

The noun-idea was more difficult, and probably followed long after. But it too was necessary for real language.

Just how it developed is harder to suggest. Yet the tendency of speech is to begin with the special and concrete nouns before working over to the general and abstract. Certainly the most special and concrete of them all are proper names, and for this reason the first nouns may have been the names of individuals. One person, it might happen, would often snore. Possibly at first in fun, others would make the same sound to refer to him. Once started, the habit of individual names might quickly spread to all the members of the band, for to have a name is to have a bit of very flattering personal property; each individual might like to have one, and each mother to have one for her child.

Again, something which could start more for playfulness than for "use" might soon come to be of value in other ways. When the band was foraging, one of them might signal his position by calling "Coo!" like a dove, to let the others know where he was.

Eventually came the union of the noun-idea and the verb-idea. It may be that a woman came back without her companion, and much troubled. All attempts at gesture failed to tell what had happened. In desperation, naturally enough and yet with a stroke of genius, she cried, "Coo-ouch!" Then they knew that he who was called Coo had been taken with a sudden pain. Such a combination of two ideas was more than mere expression of personal feeling, and more also than mere pointing-out of an individual. It was the setting of two ideas into a new relation, and thus the beginning of real language.

I like to think that the mothers may first have made and practiced language, and that for some generations the fathers still sat around merely grunting while the mothers chattered happily. At least I notice that girl-babies are still quicker to speak than boy-babies, and that they grow up in general to be the more apt talkers. Besides, there has always been in language a great deal of an illogical and emotional quality. I might say, "Women invented language, but men invented grammar."

The discovery of language was as great an event as anything that had happened. Its obvious uses, as anyone can recognize, were social—for all kinds of working and playing together. But perhaps it was greatest as a tool which more than any stick or stone gave me power over the world. For not only is language an instrument for telling thought, but it is also an instrument for thought itself. I do not want to raise that old argument of whether thought is possible without speech; but at least I am sure that thought cannot go very far without language, any more than mathematics can go very far without its symbols.

First of all, language was the great tool for classification of knowledge, and without classification of ideas my brain would have become as cluttered as a library with a million volumes and no card-index. From the beginning, every noun and verb performed an act of classification,

Barry University Library
Miami, FL 33161

drawing a mental circle around everything included within it, shutting outside all the rest. At first the circles might be few and large, but the very existence of words made the distinctions of classes clearer, and so new classifying went always further. Always I needed new distinctions, and having found words, thereafter needed still finer distinctions.

The systems of classifying are many, and this too stimulated both thought and language. At first, I should guess, the individual and the group were confused. "Leopard" might at first be like a proper name, as still one may say "The leopard is dangerous," as if there were only one of its kind. Also the first lines of classification may have been very different from those we now think proper. Let us say that *arghk* meant a danger and thus included lightning and poisonous berries, along with crocodiles, poisonous snakes, and large leopards. But *biah* might include all harmless animals, including the leopard-cub.

This would not necessarily mean that I then saw no common relation between a leopard and a leopard-cub, but it would at least tend to keep the relation a little vague. Eventually, although *arghk* and *biah* might be still retained, a word would arise to include within its circle all leopards, or perhaps all cats, large and small. Such a word would represent a classification along a new line, and thus a sharpened appreciation for a new kind of knowledge.

Classification thus became tied up with abstraction. To use the word *leopard* meant that I had in some way isolated the quality *leopard-ness* which was held in common by certain large dangerous animals and by other small harmless ones.

The greatest implement for cross-classifying arose some time later with the adjective. Every word like *blue* was an abstraction, because *blueness* never existed in itself but always as something blue. This abstraction moreover ran like a linked chain across other classifications, and meant that I made note of a common quality in such divergent things as a blue flower, a blue sky, a blue bird, and a blue eye. From such words was to spring much knowledge, and also much illusion.

There was one other great use of language in that with it I got a fine new means of happiness. Already perhaps I had danced with intricate waving of the arms on spring nights when the full moon made the night into a strange day, or like the wolf I had howled mournfully in the autumn twilight. But it was more fully satisfying to chant for all to hear:

The wind is cold,
Alas! Alas!
I am sad—

and then finish it off with a howl. Of course, anyone who could do that was probably not really sad at all, but more likely overwhelmed with pride at what a monstrous fine poem he had just made. (Yes, I am afraid, I took up vanity and hypocrisy a long time ago.)

6

I get fire, cookery, and clothing

As FOR fire, plenty of charred wood has been found in the caves of the Pekin man. My use of it is therefore very ancient, but probably came long after I had begun to wield tools and to talk. I had from the first, like most animals, a habit of communicating by sounds, and I had also that old liking for branches which easily passed over to sticks and stones. But I had nothing in my past which would make me love fire—rather the contrary.

Even from the trees I must have seen fires, and eyed them with the alarm which is common to all wild creatures, but a tropical forest seldom burns. Along the edge of the forest, however, I must have come to be familiar with grass and brush fires set by lightning. Often my bands must have fled in terror from the blaze, or even been caught in the flames.

Yet only a few lightning fires grew large. Most of them smouldered a while, blazed up here or there, and then died out. Although a vast conflagration was wholly terrifying, there was nothing terrible about a little fire, especially in the daytime when the sunlight blotted out the mysterious dancing light of the flame. I was a curious and playful creature, and in the daytime not timid. So, I can imagine, one of my bands edged nearer and nearer to a little fire, the males in front, each dubious at heart but not wanting to run before the other did. The fire did not reach out and bite them, and next time they went closer. From a little distance, the children of that band looked on, and grew up thinking of fire as wonderful, not harmful. (Even yet children so feel the fascination that they can hardly be kept from burning themselves and the whole house.)

At first, fire could have been of no "use" at all. It was just to be looked at, a strange rarity. Next, I should say, it became a plaything, when some bold one picked up a blazing branch and waved it to and fro. After that, it may have helped to build up a sense of power, as when the boldest of all chased the others with the blazing branch and scattered the whole band in panic.

With time (granting always an active and observing and judging brain) the habits of fire became known. It singed hair and burned skin. It "fed" upon dry branches and leaves. Rain and water killed it. Beneath its gray ashes it seemed to die, but often lived in some strange fashion, as a person in sleep. By wind or by blowing from the mouth it could be awakened to life. With these discoveries came a little ability to control fire. But how to kindle or create it remained for a long time as unknown a mystery as how the child first came to be within the mother.

In spite of my devotion to common sense, I am ready to agree that a rare curiosity, and a plaything, and something which cultivated my sense of power, was already of some use. But for those who are harder headed I will suggest that fire first became of conventional "use" when I learned that the killers who ranged the night were afraid of it. While the flame played yellow against the trees, the tiger circled, grumbling, but kept his distance. So, in the desperation of darkness, as the fire burned low, I put to use what I had learned by playing. I fed the fire, and kept the blaze going until the dawn.

In cold weather I must have noticed also that fire threw out a pleasant warmth like the sun's. But this was probably of little importance to me; I was well accustomed to taking the weather as it came.

More likely, however, my close alliance with fire sprang from none of these causes, but from something different and even stranger.

If it had not been for the discovery of those caves where the Pekin man lived, I would not yet have dared assume that cookery came so early. Perhaps "cookery" is a too-elegant term for what must have been the mere throwing of chunks of meat into the coals of a fire, but there is no other word.

Yet, when I think the matter over, I can see both that cookery must have come early and that it was a matter of first importance because it was tied up with a basic change of habits. In the trees I was chiefly vegetarian although eating a good many birds' eggs and some nestlings, tree-toads, grubs, and insects. Migration to the ground brought no great change. I did not develop the slashing dog-teeth and powerful jaw of the killer and meat-eater. From the evidence of my teeth throughout many centuries after coming to the ground, I must have remained just about the same kind of eater that I had been in the trees. In all those centuries, even if I came to where a bison had fallen over a cliff and lay freshly dead, I must have passed by. With teeth and jaw not much different from those I still have, I could not readily bite through the tough hide and then attack the stringy muscle beneath. The labor would have been greater than the gain, and the more practical course was certainly to go on to gather grass-seeds or pounce upon a frog. A rabbit or a partridge was about my limit.

Tools and fire changed all this. With the freshly broken edge of flint I cut and hacked through hide and flesh. With fire I broke down the tough meat of the wild animal into something which my weak teeth and jaws could economically chew. Probably I had no idea of improving the flavor, and at the beginning I may have looked upon cookery as a bad compromise which sacrificed the delightful raw-meat taste in favor of the practicality of easier chewing.

There is another point here. Cookery has usually been the woman's part. She, being weaker in jaw as well as in her other muscles, may first have grasped the utility of making fire do part of the work. At least, this is a pretty fancy!

In any case, it is fairly sure that the Pekin man cooked his meat, and no living primitive tribe has been discovered without a well-developed use of cookery. So I think that at a very early time, but following the use of stone tools and of fire, I gradually became more of a meat-eater—and the results were much more important than you might think.

Because cooked meat was a concentrated and quickly digested food, I needed to spend less time eating and lying around stupidly afterwards. That left more time for thought and for play. Again, I still could not yet move my fire easily, and so I had a strong reason to settle down at a more or less permanent habitation. Yet again, cookery developed a sense of self-restraint. Instead of merely falling to, I had to butcher, carry the meat to the fire, wait till it roasted, and then finally until it cooked. Cookery was a natural breeder of decorum, and enforced its rules of etiquette with the threat of a burned mouth.

Most important of all, as the centuries rolled on and on, love of eating meat gradually turned me into a hunter; and so, as much as any of the five, cookery set me upon the road to the future.

There is no evidence that the Pekin man wore clothing; yet I always try to keep in mind that lack of proof for something does not necessarily mean the establishment of proof the other way. Clothing, I must remember, does not resist decay, like stone-tools and charcoal and half-burned bones, and it does not show in the shape of the skull as the development of speech does.

For many reasons, however, clothing was probably the last of the five. The making of clothes and the fastening of them to the body required tools and skills which would have to be developed first.

There has been much argument (nobody of course knows for certain) about whether clothing originated as ornament, or for what are called more practical reasons, such as shelter from cold. I myself think that it began with the practical idea of protection from injury.

When I began to run on two legs, I exposed to the scratching and knocking of every bush and branch those tender parts which in other animals are carefully kept out of the way under the body. In rough, bushy country I had to be on my guard. Even so, I must constantly have suffered pain or even serious injury. As soon as I had learned to take skins from animals and to tie the ends or tuck them in firmly, I had every reason to try to shield myself.

My feet also needed protection, so that sandals may have been the second kind of clothing.

I have no wish to imply that ornament was not a primitive desire also. But in this case I rather think that what was first put on for protection came to be thought also an ornament, rather than the other way round.

Once the idea of clothing had arisen, it produced other results. One of them was modesty. The story of Adam and Eve puts it in reverse, that modesty produced clothing; but, more likely clothing produced modesty. Clothing, ornament more particularly, also became involved with all sorts of magic, and with love-making. But such ideas, like modesty, came much later. Magic was a sophistication, and love-making in those days was probably too simple to call for gewgaws.

But certainly clothing was a momentous discovery. Perhaps in the long run it has given the individual as much pleasure as cookery or speech. But it has also, like all the other four, given me great power over the world.

To protect myself I have developed shoes and boots, gloves, armor, masks, bracers, jockey-straps, hard hats, cowboy chaps, asbestos suits, and many other devices to enable me to do what otherwise I could not do, or could only do with risk. To shield me from the sun's rays have come sombreros, straw hats, pith helmets, and burnooses. To shield me from cold have come thousands of devices ranging from the primitive sheep-skin thrown over the shoulders to red flannel underwear and electrically heated suits.

In the end, protection from cold has seemed to be the chief purpose of clothing. Certainly it has enabled me to create a kind of artificial climate. Thus aided, I spread into the coldest countries, and yet remained hairless.

I, Man, thus came to know those five which have been the basis of my life ever since. In achieving them, I developed my brain and made my hands more clever. I also stored up a tradition of knowledge which one generation passed on to the next.

Having gained so much that the animals did not have, I think that I must also have begun to develop some consciousness of myself and a sense of power, to consider myself as standing off a little from the rest of things. Perhaps I was not yet Lord of Creation, but I felt on equal terms with any of the creatures. I could not fly like a hawk, but I knew I was stronger. If I was not as strong as the buffalo, I knew already that the buffalo was stupid. The leopard might seem as clever as I, and stronger too —but he was afraid of fire. Besides, few leopards would charge home against a dozen yelling, leaping men, and a volley of well-hurled stones.

It was a kind of balance of power. The leopard lorded it over the night. The buffalo ruled on the open plain. In the river-shallow there was no arguing with the crocodile. But yet I was asking no pity. I might not be the master, but at least I was taking care of myself well enough.

7

Change, and some thoughts about it

At this point, after the five basic discoveries, I have brought my story down well into what is called the Paleolithic, or Old Stone Age. Although I, Man, am frequently a pedant, I am not in this story going to use many long names, especially when a name (such as this one) is misleading. For I doubt whether stone was really more used in that time than wood or bone. The difference is that wood and bone decay readily, but stone may remain as fresh as ever. So the idea naturally enough arose that the tribes of that time used stone, and almost nothing else.

This was also the time of the cave-man, but much the same delusion exists in that connection too. Over most of the world there was little need to live in caves, and the bands probably stayed in the open, wandering around more or less and even learning to carry their fire with them. But camps left little trace in comparison with caves, which might be inhabited every winter for many generations. Thus both the ideas of the stone age and of cave-dwelling sprang largely from too much thought about the evidence available and too little thought about the evidence which was not available. But this is something which I have seen happen in historical times too, for by nature and training the scholar is likely to be influenced too much by the evidence at hand and to lack imagination to consider the evidence which may have been lost.

Yet I can realize the too-great fascination which these stone tools exert, for when I come to tell about this period, they are the first things I think of. Simple as they are, they show the way in which I gradually was changing, and my life growing more complex.

First, probably in some remote time before the use of fire, I began to make those crude and half-shaped things called eoliths, or dawn-stones. There is not much use in trying to say whether these were hand-axes, or hammers, or what. Obviously each of them was an all-round tool which was carried about and used for a little of everything. It was a roundish chunk, chipped to a rough edge on one or two sides, about the size to fit snugly into a hand. It was a formidable weapon for in-fighting, but could be used also for pounding, digging, scraping, and knocking fruit from trees. Thrown at close range, it was heavy enough, with luck, to crumple a lynx in full spring.

But as the centuries flowed along, the eolith gave way to chisels, hand-axes, scrapers, and so forth. More interesting to me, however, than the tools themselves is their evidence as to what I was learning to do. A primitive thing called a scraper is crude and not at all eloquent until you realize that it points to much else. It means not only a scraper, but a thing to be scraped, most likely a hide; therefore it means a growing ability to kill, to take off the hide, and to cure it. That is just the beginning, for a scraper also shows a knowledge of how to scrape, and a desire for scraping, and enough leisure (beyond the struggle to get food) to allow time for scraping. All this again means self-restraint and thought for the future, and it implies a certain confidence in the ways of life, because no one would be likely to go to all the trouble of scraping if he did not have reasonable hope of enjoying results of the work.

So even the existence of a crude scraper of stone shows that things were changing. Change may have been so slow that the smallest unit worth considering is an era rather than a year or a century. Even so, there was change, and I might now as well as later take up the question of how change came about, for already this involved such things as development, invention, and what is called progress. And since I am writing a story, I am particularly concerned with change, which is really the substance of any story.

Much change, I think, arose without anyone ever becoming self-conscious about it at all. Let us consider the mortar, which was an implement among early people, and even yet is used in laboratories and pharmacies.

When I first began to break nuts or pound things into a mash, the natural way to do it was to lay the nuts or whatever else on a flat rock and pound them with a stone. No rock is absolutely level and smooth, and so the material would roll or gradually slide into a hollow place. As years passed, the pounding itself deepened the hollow place, and it became a cup-like hole convenient for keeping the material in one spot. And thus, without anyone's giving any thought to the matter there was a mortar.

Another common way for the production of change is through what is usually called invention. That word is generally limited too much to the discovery of gadgets, but I mean it to include also the discovery of new ways of doing things and of new social institutions and even sometimes of new processes of art.

I shall illustrate by taking what may really be the first great invention; that is, it was possibly the first thing to spring into being by the sudden creative act of a gifted mind. In fact, though it originated well back in the Old Stone Age, I still consider it a brilliant achievement, comparable to the bow, the steam-engine, or the airplane. It was the first example of a basic idea of manufacturing.

This magnificent and world-shaking discovery was the joining together of two things, so that the whole was something different and better than either of the parts.

Whether the first joining was to produce an ax or a hammer or a spear is not of much importance. I shall assume that it was a spear. A real spear probably came into being by four steps, and took a long time. Each of the steps was important in itself, although the last was by far the most remarkable.

First, I discovered about thrusting. This was not common even among animals. They bit and clawed, or kicked, or lowered their heads and charged. Only a few, such as the snake and some long-horned antelopes used the full technique of thrusting—to lunge, recover, and lunge again. Because of this very rarity the thrust was disconcerting, besides being highly dangerous. Throwing perhaps came naturally to me, but thrusting was certainly something I had to learn, and even yet I am likely to go in slugging instead of punching. Yet in the end I learned to thrust with a stick, perhaps using it first to prod at small animals in holes. This was doubtless a notable discovery at the time.

After a while I took the rather easy second step. Many sticks naturally broke so as to leave sharp points. By accident or in play I learned that such sharp sticks hurt more and even pierced the skin easily. Then it was not much to choose sharp sticks, or to break several until I got a sharp point, or to sharpen one on purpose.

The third step was the kind in which accident plays a large part. When a tribe had fire and was using sharp sticks, sooner or later one of them was left just close enough to the fire to become hardened, or else someone accidentally chose a partially charred stick to sharpen. Such accidents might happen a hundred or a thousand times during the course of centuries before anyone saw the connection. Thoroughly stupid people might never grasp it. But in the end some clever one noticed that fire really hardened wood, so that it kept a point better. Even so, this step involved only a kind of second-rate invention, the mere taking notice of what had already happened rather than real creation.

But the fourth step was the brilliant one, and could not have happened very well by accident. I cannot see either how it could have evolved slowly over centuries, bit by bit. The only way, or at least the simplest way, to explain such a discovery is to credit it to the creative moment which comes to the gifted individual. His tribe, we may assume, had fire-hardened wooden spears, and also used sharp stone points for scrapers or knives. In a brilliant flash he saw the two combined into something new under the sun—the heaviness and sharpness of stone joined with the length and lightness and strength of wood.

The idea itself was not enough. Afterwards he had to work out some way actually to fasten stone point to wooden shaft. This again did not happen slowly over the course of centuries. The mere idea would not be passed from one generation to another, and even its original creator would not be likely, under primitive conditions, to spend year after year working on it. So we almost need to assume that the original discoverer worked out the practical side; or else with the aid of language, he passed the idea on to a more plodding and clever-handed fellow who tied the spearpoint to the spearshaft with thongs, and probably in the end took credit for the idea too.

Anyone looking back from modern times at what seems to him this very simple implement may be inclined to pooh-pooh it. But I, Man, still regard it with wonder. In it lay all the idea of the most complicated modern machines, built up by joining hundreds and thousands of parts. In making it, I grasped the essence of fabrication and assembly-line production. Moreover, the production of the first stone-hammer or spear represented an advance from zero to one, and so is in proportion something greater than all the later advances put together, for they show only an advance from one to ten thousand.

There is even something more. In fastening the two-piece implement together, I most likely tied the head to the handle with a thong. This thong thereupon became the ancestor of dowels, pins, nails, and clasps, and then later of screws, nuts and bolts, couplings, bearings, safety-valves, grease, catalysts, and all the other myriad things which exist, not to be of any direct value, but merely to hold other things together or to act indirectly through them. Symbolically, I should say also that this thong is the ancestor of many modern workmen, such as time-keepers, lawyers, and middlemen. For, like bolts and bearings, these produce neither sustenance nor pleasure in themselves, but merely aid indirectly in the working of the whole machine.

Lastly, I should say that the joining of the two things was memorable in that it forced me to face and to solve an important problem in abstraction, that is, the *idea* of joining. And most of my later development, I notice, has been tied up with the solving of abstract problems and the resulting establishment of general principles.

In all this I see the importance of leisure. If anyone was too busy merely grubbing along, he had no time to work out something new, however great its future value. So I speak out strongly against the old proverb "Necessity is the mother of invention." Necessity is, more truly, the mother of improvising and makeshift.

Even improvising and makeshift, however, sometimes led on to change; I would not rule them wholly out. Also, I say something for the importance of play, and the experiment which was often part of play. Then of still more importance was that slow unnoticed change of the kind that produced the mortar. Accident played its part too, but with accident we must assume the quickly observant and judging mind which put the accident to use. Most important of all, however, I credit that sudden creative act of the gifted one who in the flash of his brain saw something which before was not.

Whenever I get to discussing this matter of change, I find myself breaking it down into three parts. There was the change in my relation to the world around me; and second, the change within the group, or social change; and third, the change in the individual himself, involving such matters as his comfort, contentment, and happiness.

These three did not stand alone, and a change in one was often passed on to the others. Generally, I think, change with respect to the world came first.

I can show what I mean by again considering the spear. First and most obviously, it was an instrument by which I got more power over the world. With it, either by thrusting or throwing, I could kill certain animals more easily than before.

But immediately it demanded social change. A single spearman had great strength but also great weakness. Much more than a club-fighter, he faced only one way and was easily thrown off balance or outflanked. So spearmen were much stronger in a clump than separated, provided each of them stood his ground. Each also must learn what to do; there should be a point-spearman, and flankers, and a backer-up. In earlier times, when a suddenly disturbed panther charged upon the band, the best maneuver was to scatter in all directions; then the panther overtook and killed only one—or two, at most. But the spear perhaps taught a new way. If the spearmen sprang together, they might be able to stand off the panther altogether, or even to pin him down and kill him. Thus a new invention might teach new ways of living together.

Then, too, the spear affected the individual by bringing him a new and pleasing sense of power. He came also to enjoy and cherish his own well-made weapon, to take pleasure in its fine balance, and to labor over it with love, smoothing and polishing it, and even giving it a name.

8

Social revolution

I, MAN, have been telling about cookery and stone weapons as if their only importance was to give me power over the world around me. But in the end they upset my way of living within the band, a tremendous change affecting everything else which has happened since. It was simply this: that I learned about hunting, and therefore shifted gradually from a foraging-band to a hunting-and-foraging-band, which was something very different.

Even in the trees I had been, of course, a hunter in a small way; at least I hunted out grubs, and crept up stealthily to seize some insect before it took wing. On the ground I gradually went a little further, and after many centuries learned how to knock over a rabbit with a well-thrown club or stone. After I had chipped a flint into a sharp edge, I had a way to saw through the tough skins of larger animals, and to cut off chunks of the meat, tasks that were too much for my teeth. Also, as I have said, I grasped the idea of cookery.

From then on, I turned more of my attention to hunting, but for another long period I had to remain chiefly a forager, until I learned more about animals: where each was to be found, how each could be outwitted and killed, which were too dangerous or wary to be worth the risk and trouble. Once again, lack of knowledge rather than lack of tools may have held me back. For a long time I took chiefly, of the larger animals, the old or young or sick. Or, I had no scruples against eating an accidentally dead one, or the half-devoured kill of the wolf or lion. But eventually I learned the necessary lore of the hunter —to track and trail, to set snare and dig pitfall, to still-hunt from down wind, to plan the surround and the drive, to watch by the game-trail, to lie in wait at the water-hole, and a thousand other stratagems and wiles.

When I made the spear and learned to throw it, I had at last a magnificent hunting-weapon, something which put the matter on a new basis. From then on, more and more, many tribes must certainly have begun to take greater interest in hunting than in foraging. When they did so, their brains began to work in a new way.

I have already told how cookery encouraged me to settle down at a permanent campfire, and taught me something about waiting and self-restraint. Also, the whole process of learning to hunt stimulated my mind. Every day I faced new problems. I had to develop memory and judgment. I learned the need of courage and of quick decision. More than ever I learned the value of sheer intelligence, for by greater cleverness rather than by greater strength every hunter—whether fox, lion, or spearman—most easily got his dinner. Much of my life still follows the ways of thought which began as hunters' ways.

For example, hunting gave rise to sharper distinctions within the band, for it demanded unhampered power of muscle. The mothers had ranged well enough with the foraging-band, but with clinging children, they could not keep up with the hunters. In the wolf-pack, indeed, dog-wolf and bitch-wolf ran together. But the wolves were hunters by ancient instinct and long tradition. I, Man, took up hunting only in my later days, and my mothers could not, like the bitch-wolf, leave their babies in the den, and run with the pack.

So, I think from the beginning, only the fathers hunted, and thus for the first time a wide gap opened between the hunter and the keeper of the fire. What began chiefly because of the children soon grew stronger because of difference in training. Boys learned throwing, and the making and use of weapons; but girls, how to care for children and cook the meat.

Also, while the hunters were away, the mothers and children still wandered about, gathering nuts, and roots, and seeds of grasses, in their seasons. I can even imagine a long period when the hunters gorged on roasted flesh, but the mothers, who more often clung to traditional ways, still ate more of the older foods. (And even yet I observe my females deciding to have just a salad for lunch, and telling my males to eat their vegetables.)

A hunting-band, moreover, had to learn higher forms of working together, not merely the instinctive drawing together or scattering. A lone hunter worked by stealth, slowly and against odds. He waited till the nibbling rabbit at last hopped within throwing-distance; or, from down wind, he tried to creep up upon the wary goat.

But a band of hunters gained greater powers, and could stampede a bison-herd over a cliff, or lure a mammoth into a morass. Or, dividing into parties, some could drive the deer toward the waiting spears of the others.

Such co-operation did not come of itself. So the proper working of the new hunting-pack was possible only when a leader, by the right mixture of strength and cleverness, held some mastery over the others. He was, however, a leader in the simple sense, that is, he went in front, took the post of danger, and headed the attack. When a stratagem was necessary, he gave directions, and by the miraculous aid of language sent each party to its position. He might enforce his ideas upon one rebel by threat of the stone-ax, but generally he was a leader, not a driver. If his plan seemed foolish or too dangerous, the sullen silence of the others would be as good as a negative vote; or if he insisted upon his own way, he might find himself alone, facing the mammoth's rush with no flank-attackers to confuse and turn the beast—and that might be the last of him. He was no hereditary king or lord, but was leader only as long as he could lead. Even at his best any strong stand of two others might outface him. After he grew old or dull, or after wounds had weakened him, some other took his place. Thus, running with the pack taught *command* and *obey*, which are two and yet one, like spear-shaft and spear-head.

The hunter differed from the forager in this also: that he learned, not merely to defend, but to attack. I, Man came to know also the wild joy of combat and the lust of the kill, and I have not yet wholly forgotten them.

Since change breeds change, the new way of life

brought still other new habits. No longer did the people have to eat fruits and grass-seeds where they were to be found. Instead, the hunter slung the dead fawn across his shoulders, or staggered back to camp beneath the dismembered haunch of the aurochs. To the safety and comfort of the fire the mothers and children also returned from their foraging. Thus the campfire, which was also the cooking-fire, became a central point. Still at the entrance of the old caves I uncover the remains of the fireplaces, and perhaps even in those days I had begun to use some such coupling of words as "hearth and home."

With better food-supply, stronger babies were born and more of them grew up. The bands became larger. More often some families took blazing faggots, and, thus carrying fire with them, went to live near less crowded hunting-grounds. They could even move into country which had been inhospitable to foragers.

The new ways of hunting, however, did not mean that the old ways of foraging were forgotten. For this reason, famine was less likely. If hunting was bad, there were still nuts and grass-seeds. So I think of myself as then living by foraging *and* hunting, for the one was added to the other, not substituted for it.

At this stage also, I suppose, those who remained foragers were definitely at a disadvantage in competing with those who were hunters also. So early then arose that problem of the backward peoples which has dogged me ever since. If a wandering band of well-armed hunters sighted some poor foragers armed with digging-sticks and hand-stones, I am afraid that I can guess only too well what happened. I should like to think that the hunters looked upon the foragers with sudden warmth of affection as their weaker brothers in a world of beasts. But, more likely, they merely saw them as something else to be hunted; and afterwards they perhaps carried the disjointed carcasses back to the fire like any other kind of meat. For always the nature of hunters was to feel fierce loyalty and love among themselves, but to have no regard for any others.

Also two bands of hunters would sometimes sight each other. Instead of sheering off, like two bands of foragers, their new aggressive habits might urge each to approach the other with mingled daring and caution. Then, since it is the nature of most individuals to like only the familiar, the hunters on each side drew closer, seeing and disliking the differences. . . .

"Look, their spear-points are not like ours!"

"They have flat, ugly noses."

"Their hair is black. . . . Do not trust them!"

If at last they approached within shouting distance, each band grew more suspicious because the others had no language, but only made a witless chatter like squirrels scolding. Or even if they could understand the others, the words had a strange and ludicrous and suspicious twang.

Next it might go to insulting gestures, or one band might try to take away the other's fresh kill. Then spears flew and blood flowed, and hatred sprang up, to be passed on down through generations.

Thereafter, realizing themselves not to be alone in the world, each band might call itself The People and their rivals by some name such as The Strangers. And the mothers of each would tell their children that the others were little better than beasts and even worse than beasts in some ways. "Therefore, my son, never trust them, but keep the spear ready, and be quick to strike, or they strike first." For thus the way of thought is, among hunters. (And so it has been the same story ever since—ho-hum!—but also, alas!)

9

Concerning my individuals

Even when he had begun to live as hunter-and-forager, the individual had become, I think, something not so much different from what he is today. Granted that I cannot know for certain very much about what he was like in those days, still I can make some good guesses. First, I assume that he lived beneath the rule, then as later, of the elemental drives: to eat, to mate, and to defend himself. Also he must already have had qualities which he still shares with many other mammals, such as a strong love of the young, playfulness, and curiosity. Certain other traits, such as judgment and the ability to profit by trial-and-error, I assume from the making and use of even simple tools.

I wish I could remember just when I began to laugh and to weep, those most human activities. I am not sure, but I think that anyone who cooked his meat had developed far enough at least to guffaw when his comrade slipped and sat down in the mud. And any tribe with wit enough to develop language would probably soon have enough of another kind of wit to make puns. As for weeping, it is always admitted to be close to laughter, and I have no doubt that even in those days the individual did not lack reasons for weeping.

Some other qualities of the individual I would infer to be very old because I have been trying for centuries to get rid of them, and yet I seem to have them just as much as ever, if not more—pride, vanity, envy, hypocrisy, gluttony, and indifference to the suffering of others. On the contrary, there are some qualities which I have always been trying to develop and which I never get the hang of: for instance, self-restraint, foresight and placidity. I am simply not in the class of the beaver or elephant or honey-bee. Even the cat fills me with admiration and wonder at her patience before a mouse-hole. I am more nearly of the grasshopper's persuasion. In spite of Aesop and Confucius and Franklin, I am still likely to eat my apples green because I can't wait for them to ripen. Of course even the earliest individuals must have had restraint in some degree. But I think at the late date of 100,000 B. C. they must still have squandered and wasted, and lived for the moment, in a way which would be shocking even to present-day hoboes and members of café society.

Some might think that such a marked change in the general average of restraint should be called "progress." I hesitate over that word. I have noticed that every change seems to bring something of which I might well be ashamed as well as something of which I might well be proud.

Increased restraint, for instance, brought much which seems admirable—from better table-manners to fewer murders. But it also brought cruelty and torture, for only someone who has developed forethought can resist killing his enemy outright, and settle down to spread the pleasure over an afternoon. So I prefer generally to think of "change," not of "progress."

About this time my more gifted individuals began to play with thought itself. At first, that is, it may have been play, and then like so much else it came to have other values. Language must have been a chief help here, because many words were themselves adventures in pure thought.

From various things that happened, I believe that I now became able to separate out the idea of cause-and-effect. In a practical sense this was one of my most wonderful discoveries, and by thinking consciously in that way I have been able to gain control over the world at a much faster rate than before. But, as always, this discovery too worked in the opposite direction. It has led me into some stupendous errors, and to this day when I think about the matter I still get mixed up. If you get me into a corner, I can only admit that one thing happens *after* another, and whether cause-and-effect is anything more, I cannot say.

Let me show what I mean. Very early I learned that after I had a fire going in cold weather, a pleasant heat was thrown off. So I said, "Fire *causes* heat," and when I wanted heat, I built up the fire. This was something worth knowing. But also I observed that thunder came after lightning, and so I said "Lightning *causes* thunder." I know now that I was wrong, and that lightning merely *seems* to come first because it travels at the speed of light while thunder travels only at the speed of sound.

This particular matter of lightning and thunder probably did no harm, but similar illusions might be serious. Let us say, some band when in great hunger saw a magpie and soon afterwards had success in hunting. Then, by coincidence, the same thing happened again. The hunters were impressed, and retold the story, and before long came to say, "Seeing a magpie *causes* good hunting." Then in the end they would be wearing magpie feathers and thinking the magpie a guardian spirit, and following all sorts of senseless and hampering practices because they had made the original mistake.

So many mistakes have thus sprung from the misuse of cause-and-effect that I sometimes wonder if I, Man, would not have been better off if I had never thought of it. There was much in the world that I could not explain, but once I had started with cause-and-effect I felt uncomfortable in the presence of something unexplained. And so I was constantly making up explanations of things which *seemed* reasonable whether they were really true or not, and so gave me treacherous comfort.

Thus from reflections in pools of water and from shadows, from echoes, and from dreams, I got the idea of a whole Other-world. It was mysterious and did not follow the same cause-and-effect that I knew. So I assumed it the more powerful of the two worlds and really to control the common one I moved in. Language helped to give this effect, for it was always using expressions like The Tiger, which implied some great Universal Tiger or Tiger-spirit.

There is reason to think that I developed such ideas as far back as 100,000 years ago, and gradually came to believe the world to be full of all kinds of spirits: river-spirits and lightning-spirits, tree-spirits, tiger-spirits, and so on forever. There was a certain amount of terror in this idea, but there was much more comfort. The most terrifying things are those which cannot be explained, and once I had conceived of spirits I had a glib explanation for everything. I even had a ready answer for the unusual, for I thought the spirits to be much like myself, and so quite likely to be inconsistent. Besides, these spirits were very far from being all-powerful or all-knowing. I could poke fun at them behind their backs, and often enjoyed making fools of them.

About as far back as 100,000 years ago, also, some of my tribes began to bury their dead and place food and weapons in the grave. This furnishes as good proof as anyone could ask that they were already well enough convinced of the Other-world to think of themselves also as having spirits—spirits which passed to the Other-world after death, as the mind of a sleeper ranges far in dreams.

Even though I have now partially outgrown the idea of the Other-world, I still must admit that it was an amazing achievement for me to work out when I was still using stone tools, and not even very good ones. It was the first great religious and philosophical and scientific system; it dominated, for comfort and for terror, long after civilization had arisen, and was not much improved upon; even yet it is powerful.

Possibly I should tell more about this early religion,

for it occupied a large place in my life, and many heavy books have been written about it. I pass over it rather quickly, however, because I no longer believe in such hocus-pocus and cannot think that it amounted to much in my development. The rituals and dances undoubtedly gave my individuals a great deal of real pleasure, and also a great deal of false comfort, in that they considered themselves thus to gain the favor of the Other-world. But I, Man, no longer think that the beating of tom-toms and the whirling of bull-roarers built up to anything greater. Such things did not carry me on from change to change. No, the efforts of my own hand and brain did that.

If the rites and rituals and dances gave my individuals pleasure and comfort, that is enough to make such things important. But, having gladly admitted so much, I still see no reason for going into the details.

All these new ideas of religion and the Other-world were first worked out in the minds of the more gifted individuals and then were passed on gradually to the tribe as a whole. For by this time life was getting somewhat easier, and therefore a greater amount of difference was showing between individuals themselves. As the tribe grew stronger, it could give shelter to more variety. It was no longer the band of primitive foragers living from hand to mouth in the strictest sense, with the penalty of death in the leopard's claws always there for anyone who failed to do just the conventional thing.

The hunting-and-foraging was more complicated than mere foraging. The older life had put a premium upon qualities like agility, quick observation, strong digestion, and the ability to last through a starving-time. In hunting-and-foraging those qualities were still good, but there were new needs—for powerfully muscled bodies, and for cunning minds to outwit the goat and deer, and to win in open competition with the wolf and panther. Doubtless all the individuals of the band changed somewhat to meet the new conditions, and it would be even more likely that some changed more than others.

With the whole tribe more powerful, a tendency to lay on fat would not mean that an individual soon fell prey to the leopard. Instead, being better fitted to sit quietly, the fat one was posted with his spear in the ambush, while lighter-footed and more skittish youths went to drive the quarry. So at last individualism became possible, and even advantageous for the tribe.

There were the massive-built, square ones, the leaders of the hunt. When the boar charged, the fire of battle blazed in their hearts, and they sprang forward with wild cries, thrusting surely. Because they were strongest they took the best of the meat and lived well. But often they died on the boar's tusks, and in the long winters they drove themselves too hard, and perished in the cold and the starving-time.

There were the round ones too. When the boar charged, they scattered like rabbits. But they were more patient at lying in wait. In the winters they lived on their fat, and found warm places by the fire, and slept. They survived.

There were also the tall and thin ones. Most often they died as children, but if they lived, they brought something new to the tribe. When the boar charged, they trembled like leaves, but stood their ground, thrusting wildly. In the nights they lay wakeful, hearing the cries of the night-beasts, thinking vague thoughts.

The strong square ones lived always in the passing moment, and the round ones told jolly tales of great gorgings, and of dangerous hunts now safely in the past. But the tall and thin ones brooded sometimes over what was yet to come, even of death and whether anything was beyond it. Sometimes a strange power came upon them. Then they charged without fear, against the lion. The others knew that power, and bowed before its brief fury.

The tall ones talked little, but sometimes when speech came to them, their words were poetry and magic. From them came many of those sudden flashes of new knowledge: that stone might be joined to wood or that the Other-world was full of spirits.

Like the fathers, the mothers changed also. But more of them remained like the round men, for in all times the first duty of the mother, for the sake of the child within her, was to survive.

So, as the tribe grew strong, the individuals became more various. And then, since the individuals were more various, the tribe grew still stronger.

There is another very important matter about the individual: by 100,000 B. C. he had come to be physically, in some tribes at least, just about what he is today. His brain was as big as a modern one. From this time on, certainly, the question of a changing body is of little importance in the story. Instead, I must tell exclusively of changes, and often very startling ones, which resulted from my getting new ideas and discovering new ways of living. Such changes could occur in a short time, whereas a making-over of the body took very long. For example, if I had had to become a hunter of big game by developing the long teeth of the wolf or tiger, it would have taken a million years. But I could invent the spear, and perfect it, and learn its use—all in a few generations.

In brief, my greatest difference from the animals came to be that they had to adapt themselves to fit the world around them, but I was able, within limits of course, to change the world to fit myself. If the climate grew colder, each species of animal must either die, or retreat to some warmer place, or develop a thick fur. But I built fires and put on clothing, and thus created a world (close to the fire or inside the clothing) in which I lived merry as a cricket and yet hairless still.

I should like to make a last point. People usually look back with pity to these early savages. One of my philosophers once characterized their life in four famous words—poor, nasty, brutish, short.

But I am not sure that my individuals of those times called for pity. Their lives were short, yes—but for that very reason they seldom knew old age and lingering pain. They passed quickly from full strength to the quiet of death. They enjoyed all the elemental satisfactions, possibly more fully and with less worry than later people could. Not knowing a soft life, they could not long for it. The individual had some chance to do as he wished. The tribe lived by the daily excitements of the hunt, not by "work."

Such a life has, in fact, had a great charm for me ever since. Long after this time, during the centuries when the frontier was advancing across North America, thousands abandoned civilization and shared the hunting-life of the Indian tribes, but I find record of very few Indians who willingly went to live in cities.

I would not go so far as to cry sentimentally, "the good old days!" Yet I really see no reason why my individuals of that time were not as happy then as they have been at any time since. Perhaps that was the reason why the period lasted so long: not that I was slow-witted, but that I lacked the urge to change, which springs from unhappiness and discontent.

10

I become master—

IN READING stories I have noticed that sometimes the writer stops telling the tale and looks around at the situation. At this point I might do the same.

Around the year 100,000 B. C., then, I find that the most complicated form of life which I had as yet worked out was that of the hunting-and-foraging tribesmen who had developed the spear and thus become able to kill big game. At the same time they had not forgotten how to kill small game and how to gather nuts and seeds. They thus had many sources of food, and were least often overtaken by famine. Since they had developed the spear, they also were the most likely tribes to have learned the other latest devices, such as improved clothing and shelters, better control of fire and even its kindling, better tools, and the belief in the Other-world. Such tribesmen must surely have begun to feel themselves the lords of creation. But in some places probably there still were less sophisticated tribes who lived the old foraging life, were more subject to famine, and without spears could not feel themselves more than the equals of the stronger beasts.

As I look back over some of the chapters I have just written, I am at times afraid that I have made it seem as if change were simply ripping along. There certainly was tremendous change. But the units of time were also tremendous. There is no use thinking of years or even of centuries. So, if I tried to draw a rising line to indicate the change throughout my career, the line before 100,000 B. C. would look perfectly flat in comparison with the line after that date.

Actually it would not be flat, and also it would not be smooth. I feel sure that change came, not steadily, but in little jumps. For I have noticed that that is the way of change. Things were very quiet, let us say, for a hundred thousand years—until some tribe developed the spear. Then for ten thousand years there followed a time of adjustment and readjustment because the spear threw the old way of life out of balance. But eventually the balance was re-established, and life settled down again for a while. That, at least, is the way things seem to go in later periods when I know more about them.

If, about this time, there had been a philosopher on the earth with a knowledge of my long history, he might have tried to make some prophecy of the future. I think that even the best philosopher would have got it wrong. Looking over the past he might have thought in these words: "Here is a creature who is developing in certain ways, and in a million years has really totaled up a surprising accomplishment. But the process has been slow. It is, of course, not at all certain he will keep on developing in the future, but very likely he will. Since he has developed so slowly in the past, however, anyone must assume that he will develop at about the same rate during the next million years."

This prophecy, however reasonable, would have been absolutely wrong. I was just at the point of beginning to change more rapidly than anyone could have imagined from my past record.

Some of this change was undoubtedly tied up with the expansion of the individuals of the modern type known as *Homo sapiens*. My archeologists have so far failed to discover much about his earlier history, probably because they have worked chiefly in Europe. Certainly, however, from the beginning, *Homo sapiens* or his ancestors must have been living somewhere, and eventually I have every confidence that someone will find some early remains of him, most likely in Northern Africa or Western Asia.

The simplest explanation would be that he lived in some region under conditions which favored the development of his brain. Like other people he learned to make stone tools, and took up hunting. Eventually something happened. Perhaps there was a change of climate for the better, so that game increased. Or perhaps there was a new invention which yielded an increased supply of food. Either way, the numbers of the people would have increased. Then, if the climate got worse again, some of them might have been forced out, looking for a place to live. Even if the climate remained good, over-population might still occur, or any of a dozen other reasons might have set the tribes to expanding and pushing out into new lands.

Eventually all the early and more primitive individuals disappeared, although here and there perhaps they mingled with *Homo sapiens.* (Thus in parts of Europe some anthropologists think they can still trace the features of the old Neanderthal people.) But in general I can say that only *Homo sapiens* remains—in his various races, whether black, white, or yellow.

The tribesmen of this modern type entered Europe from the south, and apparently began to kill off the old Neanderthalers, who had been living there for a long time, largely by big-game hunting. These newcomers were the famous Aurignacian people, who had that curious habit of painting beautiful pictures on the walls of dark caverns where it was almost impossible for anyone to see them. Of course they probably painted pictures in the open too, but these have long since weathered away. In any case the Aurignacians were thoroughly modern people.

Their pushing into Europe was in itself a change, and it was probably a sign of some change behind them. The usual reason for the migration of a people, especially into a colder country, is that they are being forced on from behind, either by mere pressure of population or by hostile tribes.

I have my own theory about this northward migration of the Aurignacians, although I have very little evidence on which to base it. To the south about this time, there was another people of modern type. They were much like the Aurignacians in most ways, but they seem to have been the first to develop a certain new weapon—as much better than the spear for hunting and fighting, as the spear had been better than the club. By means of it they could kill more animals, and thus their numbers would increase. Then being better armed, they could expand into any hunting-grounds they wished to occupy, driving all their kindred tribes before them. Such an invention at that time might cause as much upheaval of old ways of life and as much disturbance and shifting of population as the Industrial Revolution produced in modern times. When I consider this new invention, I really become lost in admiration of myself—at my own ingenuity in discovering something so much more effective than anything before it, and at the same time so much more complicated.

This new invention was the bow, and all that goes with it.

Its complication and my eternal wonder in it rest in this: that it is composed of bow, string, and arrow, no one of which is worth anything by itself. Yet combined, the three become a curious and deadly engine. In its strangeness and in its nature too, it reminds me of an electric transformer which takes in current at low voltage and sends it out at crackling high voltage. So, by pulling back the bow-string, I can store up all the energy in the bent bow, and then release it all into the arrow in a fraction of a second.

The bow is the more wonderful to me also because I cannot see any series of developments by which it could have evolved bit by bit. Some tribes have used a bow-drill for kindling fire, but this would not seem to help matters; a bow-drill is more complicated than a bow-and-arrow, and probably developed from it. I can imagine a bow with a string to be twanged as a musical instrument, but this also seems something which developed from the bow-and-arrow. A twig held in one hand and bent back with the other throws sticks or pebbles, and this might yield some suggestion, but it is a long way from being a bow. So also were those two early inventions: the spear-thrower and the sling. These, certainly, were like the bow in being mechanical devices to aid throwing, and the sling had a further resemblance in using a thong or cord. But just as the spear-thrower and sling were not so effective as the bow, so too they did not resemble it closely enough to give much suggestion for it, and even their way of applying the power was different. As often, language showed the essential distinction. The old word *throw* served for the two earlier weapons; but, having become bowmen, most of my peoples developed the new word *shoot*.

Possibly enough, the first bows were playthings, but they were not less complicated for that. There were not even, I would point out, many materials at hand to suggest a bow. A miniature spear might give the idea for an arrow, but no tribe would have miniature spears, except perhaps as children's playthings. The tribesmen must have learned about thongs and the tying of knots to be able to fasten spear-head to shaft, but a much stronger and longer thong was needed for a bow-string. And a springy stick was hardly part of the common stock; a spear-shaft should be stiff, not limber.

So again, as with the spear itself, I think that the simplest way out is to suppose the sudden flash in the creative mind. This inventor of the bow thus did as much to change the course of history as anyone before or after him. And here I might as well leave off discussing the origin, which I can admire but cannot solve, and pass on to what the new invention accomplished.

First of all, it was a hunting-weapon to be used against middle-sized game. With an arrow there was too much chance of missing a squirrel or rabbit or quail, and so I usually continued to use other devices for small game. For the largest game also, the bow was not so useful; it could not easily bring down mammoth or hippopotamus, and the earlier bows were probably not effective even against bison. But against everything from sheep to stag it was by far the most deadly weapon I had ever owned.

You will notice also that animals of this size were the most efficient for food. It was hard to feed a whole tribe with squirrels and rabbits. On the other hand, most of the flesh of a mammoth might spoil before it could be eaten, so that the great labor and risk of killing one was largely wasted. Besides, no hunting-ground supported many mammoths, and they reproduced slowly. But sheep, deer, and cattle were at once small enough to be plentiful, and large enough to yield a good supply of meat.

More food meant more babies growing up, and that meant over-population. Then the tribesmen with bows wandered into new hunting-grounds, and found that an arrow worked as fatally on a spear-armed hunter of another tribe as on a deer. Secure in this, they might undertake fairly good imitations of wars of occupation and extermination. (Thus the bow became also the great weapon of war. Throughout tens of thousands of years every military system either depended on the bow, or carefully worked out shields and armor or other means of defense against it. The last great day of the bow was not to pass until September 9, 1513, A. D., when the English archers overwhelmed the Scottish spearmen with feathered death at Flodden Field.)

But the bow did still more. It was effective also against wolf, bear, and tiger. For the first time, probably, I began to cease avoiding those animals, and to hunt them down and kill them. The bow was particularly good against them because it could be used from ambush and at safe distance. Moreover, the wounded beast was likely to start biting the arrow instead of looking for the concealed hunter who had shot the arrow. And in the end, the arrow-wound was usually so deadly that the beast often seemed to escape, and yet died eventually. Thus I could begin to take direct action against my competitors, and slowly to wipe them out.

The bow (or the spear-thrower, if that came first) also introduced the highly fruitful idea of moving parts. From such beginnings eventually came all implements and machines which move within themselves by means of such devices as shuttles, pendulums, pistons, springs, and wheels.

With a bow in my hand and the skill in my brain to use it, my sense of power leaped suddenly to new heights. Let the lion beware! Not only did I feel myself lord of the world, but also I was in excellent position to enforce my lordship.

Still another change—and a basic one—came with the bow. In all previous fighting between individuals, whether with teeth or club or spear, the chief advantage had lain with sheer power and weight. But the bow was a weapon of skill. Little difference, any longer, whether one bowman's arm was stronger than another's! Any bowman could shoot an arrow hard enough to kill the brawniest club-fighter of the tribe. True, the bow thus became also the coward's and the assassin's weapon, and probably big tribal bullies said the same things against it that armored knights were later to say against villainous gunpowder. But fact remained fact. If the bow did not make all men alike strong, it was at least a disturbing challenge to the ancient dictatorship of brute force.

By and large, I do not think it too much at least to advance the theory that the bow, while at first it seemed to reinforce the old hunting-and-foraging life, in the end made that life impossible. It was perhaps too efficient, and threw off the balance. I, Man, began to be able under many conditions to kill animals faster than they could reproduce. Thus that way of life which I had built up through so many thousands of years began to tumble down, and like someone who has stumbled at the top of a hill I had to run faster and faster not because I wanted to, but just to avoid falling on my face.

11

—and am acknowledged

My next great adventure followed, in centuries, long after the bow. Yet in my whole scale of time the two are close together. In this same period, which counts as the last part of the Old Stone Age, many other changes occurred also. There was in fact a definite speeding up.

For instance, I was learning about how to kindle fire in various ways. I was also making better tools. I had discovered about using needles, and so was probably making myself better clothes. Certainly I was making beads and wearing ornaments. I was setting out to enjoy life in other ways too: by using pipes and whistles of bone to play some kind of simple music, and by inventing rituals and dances.

About this time also I, Man, seem to have taken more to the water. This was not only of practical advantage, but also it built up my sense of power. My upright posture had from the beginning made swimming hard for me. Nevertheless I had probably learned early enough, by watching the bear, to scoop up fish from shallow pools; and because my fingers were always ready to explore crannies, I invented the trick of searching under banks and between rocks and grabbing the fish that were hiding there. But now came the use of hook-and-line, and of harpoon. Also, from a mere floating log which I straddled, I got the idea for a log hollowed out by fire and stone-ax, and that was a dug-out canoe. With it the hunters crossed large rivers easily, and even traveled along them. Soon also someone floated down a river, and paddling out across the quiet bay at its mouth made the first momentous voyage on salt water. Having lost the ape-like fear of water, the hunters went exploring upon mud-flats, or were left stranded there between tides. There is an old saying: "He was a brave man who first ate an oyster!" I should say rather that he was an ingenious one. But, no matter what he should be called, he made a beginning, and from that time shellfish of all kinds came to be a favorite food.

But the chief adventure of this time was something much more exciting even than the cracking of the first oyster. Once again, naturally, there is no record of how it happened, and I shall merely have to work out the story as best I can.

I, Man, from very early times had known the wolf. While I was still a forager, his packs may sometimes have hung on the flanks of my bands, cutting off a straggler, or snapping up a baby, as still happens in India. After I became a hunter, my bands and the wolf-packs must have lived in something like armed neutrality; each was too clever and dangerous for the other to hunt, and it was easier for each to prey upon more stupid and safer animals.

I do not know just where the next step occurred. I think it was well to the south in some warm country, for in the northern forests he was a big-boned and long-fanged fighter—"that gray beast, the wolf of the weald." When I suddenly came upon him in the oak-glade, he stood bristling, or even sprang at my throat. But in hot jungle and desert-scrub, he was smaller. When he saw me, he scuttled with tail between legs, as a beast should before a spearman.

Then I invented the bow. After that, I had more meat than ever, and perhaps killed off so much game that the wolf went hungry. In the evenings I began to see his eyes shining, as he crept up close to the fire, and I heard him crunching hungrily at the half-picked bones which I in my wastefulness had thrown away. I was not afraid of him; he was not even worth an arrow. Perhaps out of my riches, I even threw the poor wolf a bone, with a lordly gesture. (For I was flattered to have a hanger-on, and I have always loved doling out charity, after I myself was full of good meat.)

Then, being hungry, he began to turn up before it was dark, to see what pickings could be had. I let him gnaw on the sheep's head and guts. He kept his distance, and learned to judge for himself how far I could throw a stone, and whether I was going to throw one. We got along rather well because we thought much the same about various matters, and had really much in common. We both hunted in packs; we spiced our courage with cowardice; we both hated all the slinking and self-sufficient cats; we ate much the same food; and both of us had intelligence. Often as I looked at him sitting with alertly cocked head, I must have said in thick accents, "Why, he looks almost human!"

Then, too, I sometimes found a lost puppy in the forest —a roly-poly and trusting bit of fur which wiggled on its fat stomach and looked up with big eyes. I lowered the raised ax and brought him to the camp. He played with the children for a while. When he grew his fangs, a wilder light began to glow in his eyes. Then perhaps he snapped at a child or eyed a baby too minutely, and the long-delayed ax crashed down. More often he merely slipped off to join the gray circling ones at the edge of the firelight. But such a wolf was never quite the same. He crept closer to the fire than the others, and remembered the children who had patted him.

Yes, as centuries slipped by, we got to know each other better. I was the leader always, chiefly because I could think more quickly and clearly. I was the cleverer hunter. Following my band, he often ate the leavings of my kill; I rarely was forced to eat his. I dominated him—by being taller and looking down, by the miracle of fire, by my fearful power to detach a stone or arrow from myself and strike from far off. (He never quite understood about this, and even yet any normal dog scuttles off when I even pretend to pick up a stone.)

Yet he had gifts that I admired too. He ran faster. When a deer escaped into a thicket where I lost the trail, he went to it directly by his own private miracle. Also, I blundered in the dark, but he got along as well by night as by day. I admired his great power of jaw too, by which he even cracked bones. This matter of the bones was still another point at which we fitted well together, for he could eat what I most often threw away.

One thing else brought us together and gave me the leadership. Ever since I had learned to talk, I had tried speaking to animals and things. "Have pity!" I cried to the lightning. "Fly well, little one!" I whispered as I loosed the arrow. But only when I began to talk to my new hanger-on did I get much response. He had the clever mind to understand, and the ear for tone. When I rapped the captured puppy over the snout, I said "No!" without thinking. After a while, I noticed that merely to say the word was enough. This was wonderful! At first he only snarled and howled in reply; at last he learned to bark, but that was the closest his stiff throat could ever come to talking.

Soon also, those gray shapes in the twilight began to pay me back many times over for the poor leavings I threw them. Their sudden outcry in the night let me know that tigers were prowling close, and I had time to throw dry sticks on the fire. When he was following and I ran foul of a she-bear, his quick snap at her heels turned her and let me get an arrow into her flank. Most of all, the pack joined in my hunt; being natural hunters, they learned when to crouch silent, when to follow by scent, and when to leap forward in full cry on the trace of the wounded stag.

It is a strange part of my story, hardly to be imagined, if it had not really happened. There is much more to it perhaps than I have told. I have always loved puppies, the mothers and children especially. And the faster growing-up of the puppies was important. A little child might be the master and protector of a young puppy, but in two years the full-grown dog (now I may call him by that name) felt himself the protector of the child. Thus by mutual give-and-take we grew together, although it was, I think, more by slow coming closer of the band and the pack than by the taming of pets.

As for the changes that the dog brought to my life—there was something of "practical" advantage, although this was by no means the equal of what the bow had brought. He helped with hunting, and thus insured a fuller food-supply. In the starving time, he also might become food-supply himself. As a scavenger, he kept the camp-sites a little more sanitary and less smelly, but I was not at all conscious of such details. As a watcher also he brought me a new security. Of more importance, I think, he served as an example. If I could gain power over one animal, I might over another, and so the way was pointed out to much in the future.

But most of all, the dog brought actual pleasure to my individuals. He at last gave proof of what I must often already have asserted: that I was lord over the animals. In his eyes (and how it has flattered me ever since!) I imagined myself to be a god.

So, as the centuries passed, the hanger-on came to be watchman, and fellow-hunter, and friend—and crept in closer to the fire. (And still he lies by the fire, importantly cocking an ear at a strange sound, then deciding it is only the boy next door coming home, falling asleep to dream ancient dreams of chasing tigers, and awaking to eye suspiciously that newcomer, the house-cat.)

Then at last I might have thought myself more fortunate even than before—with bow in hand and dog at heel, in woodland and glade, to live merrily forever. But it was not to be.

12

"What genius I had in those days!"

BY NOW, I, Man, was entering into a stage of growth when, if ever, I can think well of myself, and even cry with my Englishman: "What genius I had in those days!"

Now that I am getting down to such recent times, I can begin to date more accurately. Scholars, who always make a virtue of being "conservative" and using smaller figures instead of larger ones, seem to think that the beginnings of this new stage may be as early as 8,000 B. C. When they give such a figure it is enough to make a common-sense person like me think that the date is at least 10,000 B. C. But I, Man, am no one to argue about a thousand years more or less, and have been on the earth too long to consider such a little matter as making much difference.

The first great revolution in my life (after I really was Man) had arisen when I became a hunter and came to depend more upon hunting than upon foraging. A second great revolution now began; I discovered about producing food, and thus came gradually to support myself chiefly by raising crops and keeping animals.

Again the new discoveries did not fully displace the older ways, but were merely added to them. Even yet, when people go to gather wild blackberries or hazelnuts, they are back at foraging, the earliest way of life. Though hunting is no longer important, fishing remains a great industry, and fishing is merely a special kind of hunting.

The discovery of food-production was a matter of such importance that nothing I have done since then equals it. It supplied the basis of all civilization. Yet, as sometimes happens, this great discovery scarcely seems as difficult as some smaller ones. The cultivation of wheat could develop in easy stages from foraging, and the taming of sheep from hunting.

Naturally therefore it would be very hard, even with much more knowledge than I now have, to say exactly where and when. The two ways of producing food probably developed over the period of some dozens of centuries, and perhaps arose independently in more than one place, as different tribes gradually came to understand and control the plants and animals around them.

As to why the change occurred, there are of course the two usual theories. The number of people, some say, increased; therefore, they had to make a region yield more food or else starve. Or, others say, climate changed, and a scarcity of game was the same as an increase in the number of people. The holders of this second theory have behind them the certainty that all Northern Africa dried up gradually about this time, only the Nile valley and a few oases remaining habitable.

Both of these explanations seem to me much too mechanical, although some such theory is excellent to account for my descent from the trees. But by 10,000 B. C. my tribespeople were no longer half-apes to be shoved about only by blind forces like over-population and lack of rainfall. Instead, they had learned a good deal about controlling the world around them; they had come to have complicated desires, and knew much about satisfying their individual whims. If I could get at the truth, I would not be surprised to find that the real motives behind the first steps toward this new way of life were personal and even frivolous. (America, I remember, was discovered because of the desire for spices, not by people seeking to increase their supply of bread and meat.)

No one is sure whether the cultivation of plants or the taming of the food-animals came first. But a book is like a parade; one thing must come before another. So I shall here take up cultivation, and go on to the animals later.

Even while they were still wandering about as foragers, my tribespeople were discovering much which would be essential when they became cultivators. They learned the tricks of place and time. In the heat of summer they looked for blackberries in the gullies; a little later, grass-seed was ripe in the meadows; after the first frosts, chestnuts lay on the hillsides.

Merely by being dependent upon plants, they must have noticed much, even if they could not put it to use for a while. They saw the green shoots droop in the heat, and freshen after the shower. In a land of dry summer they noticed the grass sprouting after the first rains of autumn. Thus they learned of the "water of life."

Also they came to know the simple fact of growth from seeds. In many books there is much to-do about this business of seed, but I suppose this to be because it is tied up with sex, and any such matter gets even scholars unduly excited. In later days certainly the idea of seed became involved with life-and-death, the dying god, resurrection, and the Other-world; but I think that these complicated religious ideas came long afterwards. Actually there were few matters more obvious than the growth of plants from seeds. Anyone pulling up a shoot of wild oats or barley often saw what was left of the seed—the root coming from it in one direction, the stalk in another. Some plants, like beans, even made public display by bringing the halves of the seed up on their shoots above ground. I should imagine that I learned the poorly kept secret of the seeds quite easily and early, long before I put it to any use, and long before I knew much about the reproduction of animals, or even my own.

Foragers also learned another essential trick which they passed on. A great trouble with the earliest foraging life was that it was likely to be a feast or a famine. When the grass-seeds ripened, there was suddenly more food than could possibly be eaten, even though deer and bison and people all came crowding in. But in a little while the heads opened and the seeds fell scattering to the ground, where only the quail and mice could gather them. So it went also with the other foods. In summer and autumn, the early foragers gorged, and laid on fat to help them survive on the slimmer and slimmer pickings of winter and spring. But eventually, from the example of many animals, they learned to lay away a surplus, not on their own ribs, but by hiding nuts and acorns and grass-seeds in rock-crannies or by burying them on dry hillsides.

At first and for a long time my foragers gathered all their food in competition with others. Quail ate the berries; bison grazed upon the ripening grass; swine rooted at the acorns. But gradually, especially after learning the trick of storage, the people must have begun to think of these others as intruders and interlopers. Then began a new way of speech:

"Let us set a boy to scare the birds away from our trees!"

"We must camp tonight where the fire will keep the buffalo away from our meadow."

Once let a people have such ideas as "our" fruit-trees or meadow, and they had taken a first step toward agriculture.

Thus first perhaps I took the plants under my care, protecting them against other foragers and keeping them for myself. Then also I learned to protect them against other plants, clearing away the bushes that were choking out the young fig-tree. A little more complicated still, my wiser ones came to know that trees and grass needed protection from the people also. If anyone broke the branches to gather the fruit, there would be less fruit the next year. This meant thinking for a year ahead, but such forethought was no longer beyond their powers. So they kept the youngsters from carelessly building up the fire against the trunk of a date-palm, and pointed out the folly of holding a dance right in the middle of a likely looking stretch of sprouting grass.

Such actions helped maintain the natural growth, and saw to it that the tribe got a good share of the food. From this stage to certain kinds of primitive farming was not far or difficult, as when tribespeople in tropical countries merely cleared away the other growth and encouraged the natural patches of yams to spread farther and produce more. But elsewhere matters were not so simple, and especially in those parts of the world which were to be of greatest importance in my story.

In most places the essential trick of agriculture was the actual planting of the seed. Of course, a kind of planting happened by natural means all the time, and it could happen also by accident, or as a ritual if someone buried seed with magic ceremonies to cause better growth of wild plants. Yet, eventually, on some particular day, someone must have planted a seed in hope of reaping a crop later, burying it a little way in the earth for the simple and practical purpose of hiding it from the crows and mice.

I can never know who that person was. Because women were the cultivators in primitive tribes, most people would suppose the first planter of a seed to have been a woman, but I see no certainty even of that. I shall also never know just what kind of seed it was. Here, however, I am willing to make a few guesses. In doing so, I shall have to become something of a romancer or poet, but they often get closer to truth than scholars do.

First of all, it would not have been the seed of a tree, for trees take too long to grow. It was probably not wheat or barley, for those grains offered special problems, as

I shall point out. Moreover, I doubt whether it was anything really basic as food. Actually my guess would be that it was something rare and tasty, something for which people, or a person, might have a special craving.

Considering all possibilities, as a poet of course, I nominate some kind of melon. That is just the kind of food which someone might want to have more of. He, or she, could easily find and recognize the large seeds. Then, if anyone made the experiment of planting them, they came up with easily recognizable leaves. This made it simple to clear away the other plants, as a forager might already have learned to do. Once started, the melon-vine grew rapidly and shaded out much of the other growth. Before long, even from one seed, there was a long running vine, and after no great length of time it blossomed. As the blossoms shriveled, anyone watching them noticed the little melons, and his mouth watered in anticipation. They grew fast. If the seeds were planted close to camp, the dogs kept deer and goats away until the melons ripened. The returns from even one melon-seed might thus be definitely worthwhile, yielding a delicacy hard to come by otherwise, whereas the return from even a hundred grains of wheat or barley would not produce enough food to be important.

Thus, I think the garden came before the grain field. The tendency would be to plant the garden for dainties (and unconsciously, for vitamins) before depending upon cultivation to furnish the main support of life, which among most tribes came from hunting at this time. As Biblical tradition had it, the half-starving Hebrews remembered the fleshpots, the bread, and the fish of Egypt, but hungered even more for "the cucumbers, and the melons, and the leeks, and the onions, and the garlic." And in the same tradition, God at the beginning planted a garden eastward in Eden; he did not sow a barley field.

Yet before long, there were barley fields too, and wheat fields. I shall write in terms of wheat, because it may have been grown as early as barley, and in the end was to become more important.

Some of the natural wheat fields must have produced a rich supply of food. Moreover, it kept well, and was easy to store away. Some tribesmen must have begun to depend largely upon the harvest of native wheat, and at the same time may have grown melons and onions in their gardens. But wheat scarcely repaid the trouble of planting seed by seed, or even hill by hill. Its sprout was not easily distinguished from other grasses, and so it could not well be weeded. I had to discover still a final trick before I reaped the full reward of grain.

Curiously, there were two solutions to this final problem, and I cannot say which one came first. The two were suited to different kinds of country, but seem equally old, so far as I can yet learn.

The first was the solution for a country where the soil was naturally moist enough either from good rains or from the yearly overflow of a river, as in Egypt. Here again my cultivation of a garden gave me suggestions. Anyone planting even a hill of melons would be likely to give the seeds a decent start by clearing away the natural growth for a few inches. The easiest way to clear it would be to dig the soil with a sharp stick or stone, which after a while would be specially made as a hoe. The digging itself actually helped, by loosening the soil for new roots. To prepare a grain field you merely expanded this tiny cleared space. Laboriously digging with the hoe, you cleared the ground and overturned and loosened it until at last the soaring hawk saw something new—the dark earth of a tilled field. Then at the proper time you planted wheat thickly. With luck, it came up vigorously all at once, choked out most of the other growth, and made a wheat field.

But in a dry country there was another way. This was perhaps an easier one, so that grain-growing may have begun in some land of scanty rain like Syria. For in dry country there was little natural growth, and you could plant the wheat on ground which was nearly bare to begin with. Then the trick was to bring the water of life to the seed by some kind of irrigation—either carrying the water in a gourd, or diverting the water of a spring or stream to flow upon the field. Then, when the grain sprang up quickly, there was little other seed to grow against it, and again it made a wheat field.

In the end the whole cycle of grain developed, and built itself into one of the great human rhythms. First the ground was made ready, and then the seed planted. It was watered, if need be; it was watched and protected through summer. Then came the great days of harvesting and threshing, and the grain was laid safely away. Afterwards, the seed was set apart from the grain to be eaten, and was saved, even though the children went hungry. At last, when the storage-pits were low, then the ground was made ready again, and the cycle began once more.

I can only guess what might have happened if potatoes or yams or taro or maize had been native to Egypt and Southwestern Asia, but I am sure at least that history would have been very different. As things worked out, however, the way that I, Man, was to go depended upon the cultivation of two of the grasses which are called grains, and my future (this is not guesswork, but it is plain in the record) was in the hands of those peoples who in their early years learned how to grow wheat and barley, and to adjust their lives into that pattern.

13

More genius still!

By this time the dog had been domesticated for at least several thousand years; next came sheep, goats, swine and cattle. I name them as a group, not only because they were all tamed in the same general period, but also because I chiefly prized them as food. In fact, all of them had been commonly hunted for their meat during many centuries before they were tamed.

Since the sheep has changed more from its wild form than any other of these animals, that is some reason to think that it was the first of them to come under my control. So, to get some idea of what may have occurred, I shall imagine the situation of a particular tribe, roughly around 10,000 B. C.

This tribe inhabited, let us say, a range of low mountains surrounded by a desert plain. On the mountain-slopes the tribesmen gathered seeds and fruits, and killed some small game, such as quail and conies; but their larger game, and a chief food-supply, was the wild sheep. When good rains fell and the grass grew tall, the flocks were numerous enough to bring forth a thousand lambs. The tribesmen were able to kill a hundred sheep and lambs a year. Wolves, panthers, foxes, and eagles killed the other nine hundred, for in the long run lack of pasture prevented the flocks from increasing.

This situation, with the tribesmen killing a hundred sheep was stable, and had continued for a great many generations of men and even more generations of sheep. It suffered of course from local cycles. A series of good years produced more grass, and therefore more sheep, and therefore more wolves, panthers, foxes, eagles, and tribesmen. And then after a series of dry years there would be fiercer competition for food, and some shrinking of numbers all around. But such changes were mere ebb-and-flow.

The hunters also were often wasteful. When game was plentiful, they killed more than they needed, and ate only the choicest cuts. Or they might corner a flock in the angle of a cliff, and slaughter a dozen in the wild excitement of killing. Such wastefulness made no difference, for at most the tribesmen did not kill nearly as many as the wolves and panthers did.

Eventually, however, something happened to change the balance. Let us say, the tribesmen were learning the use of the bow-and-arrow, and steadily becoming more skillful. Their yearly take of sheep rose to two hundred, and then to five hundred. In turn their own numbers increased, as more and more fat and healthy babies played by the campfires. Then in a few years the boy-babies had become hunters, and were killing still more sheep. Before long, even in years of good grass, more sheep were being killed than there were lambs being born. Bowmen harried the flocks by day; wolves and panthers, by night; the surviving sheep grew more wary.

Then the prosperity of the tribe shifted to depression. The hunters came home empty-handed and hungry. The mothers ranged for berries and dug for coarse roots which they had scorned in the days of fat mutton. The children moped by the fires, their ribs showing. Then, if measles or small-pox struck the weakened people, they died until only a few were left.

After that, the sheep in turn increased, and the whole cycle started over. Such things probably happened not once, but often, and in many places. Sometimes, indeed, the starving bowmen may have harried the flocks so continually that the sheep were wiped out.

But I, Man, though sometimes stupid, am not altogether or always stupid. Eventually the hunters saw farther than the points of their own arrows. Older tribesmen, who had lived through a cycle of poor hunting, began to frown upon young blades who killed sheep just for the fun of showing their marksmanship. There was something else too. In the old days, when the tribe had killed only a hundred sheep and the other flesh-eaters had killed nine hundred, the tribesmen had no feeling of ownership. But when they were killing most of the yearly sheep-crop, they began to feel that the wolves and panthers were poachers—just as other people, probably about the same time, were beginning to feel the bison and deer to be intruders upon "our meadow." So the bowmen began to hunt down wolves and panthers also.

In the long run a hunter, living so closely in contact

with the sheep, developed new feelings about them. He learned their habits, and came to recognize individual rams and old ewes. He learned also that he did better to kill quietly and efficiently, without throwing the whole flock into wild confusion. So from behind his rock, he carefully picked out a fat young ram on the edge of the flock, and brought it down with so surely placed an arrow that the creature did not even have one bleat left. Then he walked forward quietly to pick up his kill, and the other sheep, who by then had seen the tribesmen many times, merely sprang off to a moderate distance and returned to their feeding not greatly alarmed. (So even yet on the African veldt the lions every night prey upon the zebras, but by day the lions and zebras remain in full sight of each other, neither paying the other much attention.)

At last—and it was a great moment in history—a tribesman passed over a mental divide. He thought, not "the sheep," but "our sheep."

Once the tribe as a whole had come to think of "*our* sheep," they could begin to practice a kind of game-preserving, which is a long step toward domestication. Then they spoke in new phrases:

"Spare the ewe with the lamb!"

"A panther has killed some of our sheep—let us go and hunt him down!"

"Spare the lamb, that it may grow larger!"

Perhaps they made up proverbs, and the graybeards nodded sagely:

"Dead ewes breed no lambs!"

"A lamb today is a ram next summer!"

After a generation or two the tribesmen could move on from the simple idea of protection:

"Kill that wary ram who is always the first to run when we approach!"

"This lost lamb is only a mouthful for eating. Let us keep him with us tonight, so that the fox will not get him, and by daylight his mother may find him."

"The wolves are harrying our sheep. Let us build a fire on the hillside tonight, and keep the wolves off them."

"Is there greener pasture already on the western slope? When we hunt today, let us work our sheep in that direction."

Thus it went for a century or two, and the sheep also changed. To kill off the wariest leaders of the flock was natural enough for hunters; but it had more results than they imagined. Not only was the leader gone, but he had no more chance to pass on his wariness to more lambs. Against moderately clever hunters like the panthers, the wariest sheep survived, and the flock grew more and more wary. Against really clever hunters like my tribesmen the wariest died soonest, and the flock grew more docile and stupid. Finally the sheep did not even think for themselves, and the flock existed only under my protection.

Thus, step by step, so gradually that no one could have told just when it happened, the tribesmen ceased being hunters of sheep—and became shepherds.

So simply told a story perhaps makes everything seem too easy. Even the gradual domestication of a flock of sheep demanded very complicated thinking. "Kill and eat!" is the simple rule for beasts and hunters alike. "Protect, nourish, and then kill!" involved new ideas and many restraints. There had to be the restraint of the wise upon the foolish who killed more than was needed, or killed for fun. There had to be the restraint to go hungry, rather than to endanger the lamb-crop for the next year. Someone had to grasp far-sighted ideas: such as killing off the wilder individuals of the flock and hunting down the wolves and panthers.

Just how much the keeping of pet lambs may have helped is hard to say. But the sheep has never been a house animal, and in general the keeping of a pet gives rise to an individual tame animal, not to a domesticated breed.

Of the other food-animals, the goat was of much the same habit of life as the sheep, and so was probably domesticated in the same way.

The story of the swine seems to be somewhat different, and more resembling that of the dog. For, like the dog and even more so, a pig was a natural scavenger, and once there was a rich piling-up around the edges of a camp, the wild pigs would be tempted in to eat it. Again as with the dog, when I was well fed, I did not grudge the pig what I had already got rid of. Since he did no harm, but rendered some service as a scavenger, I did not bother to chase him away, and even my dogs grew used to him. Being foolishly bold, the younger pigs wandered in close, caring for nothing else so long as they found food. Before long, when I wanted pig-meat, I might find a well-fed porker snoring comfortably not a hundred feet from the fire, and stealing up, I might put a spear into him before he even awoke. Thus the pig came to be, not like the sheep to be guarded in the field, but more like the dog, to be one who lived close to me, eating the leavings and often even wandering in and out of the house. Like the dog also, I think, he never had to be tamed, but really domesticated himself for the privilege of rooting through my garbage and growing fat upon whatever else I threw him. Thus he sold his freedom for a comfortable life. And who is to say whether or not he was foolish?

With cattle there were many special problems. They did not, like dogs and pigs, naturally seek my camp. In their habits they were somewhat like sheep and goats, but with one very important difference. When approached, instead of stampeding in flight, they were likely to lower horns and charge. (Even yet, a cowboy on foot cannot herd range-cattle, and no one can claim that a bull is more than half-domesticated.) Of course, as with sheep, after the hunters had hung on the flank of the herd for centuries, even the bulls might come to pay them no great attention. But quite possibly cattle were never more than half-tamed until long after the time when the sheep-flock was well under control.

By such a time, moreover, the hunters may have known about the domestication of sheep and goats, so that they had a model toward which to work. They may have set out to kill off the wilder ones systematically, and especially to get rid of most of the bulls. Also, among most cattle, the bulls withdrew from the herd for part of the year. During that time my tribesmen had a better chance to come to terms with the gentler cows and calves. As with sheep, the hunters may have given protection from wolves, and may even have urged the herd toward better pasture.

There is another point, and indeed this may be the most important one. By this time some of my tribes may have been raising crops of grain, and thus they had something to tempt cattle, much as the leavings of a hunters' camp tempted dogs and swine. Especially in time of drought and scanty grass the herds must have come pushing in until they were a nuisance, or even a menace. Once the grain was harvested, however, the starving cows could graze on the stubble, and might even be tempted by doles of grain.

Again, in some way, hard as I find it to suggest how, the cattle became dependent upon me. The cow even became friendly, although the bull stopped short at armed truce. Even beyond this, my relationships with cattle remained complex. There were range-cattle herded in the open like sheep, half-wild and dangerous. But there were also byre-cattle, so tame that a child could drive them in and out to pasture.

Little though I know for certain, I would yet venture an opinion that cattle were tamed later than the other food-animals, for they are more dangerous and difficult, and seem most to call for the temptation of special food, which only the farmer could supply.

Thus I consummated a revolution—by taming the food-animals and by learning to grow grain. The greatness of the two-horned triumph lay in this: that at last I,

Man, worked along with earth and sun and rain to *produce* food. No longer did I merely wander here and there to collect or to kill what earth and sun and rain had already brought forth, competing for flesh against the wolf and the lion, and for seeds against the cattle and the quail, existing from day to day, often uncertainly. Although it can all be told in a little space, still this matter of producing food changed my ways of living, and also my ways of thinking, possibly as much as hunting had once changed them long before. Most of my later achievements can be considered merely natural developments from this basic discovery, made in that time when genius stirred within me.

14

Change breeds change

Once the pinnacle of my life had been the camp of hunters who ranged the forest with bow and dog. But now it became the little settlement of villagers who raised grain and kept flocks and herds.

You must get away from any modern distaste for the village in order to appreciate the greatness of these first ones. Even the word should scarcely be used. Though *village* comes closest to describing the actual settlement, it gives quite a wrong idea about the minds and feelings of the people. There were then no cities which generation after generation drained off the brighter boys, and there was also no long tradition holding the villagers to their dull and stolid ways of life in subjection to the city. Instead, each village itself was a metropolis, for there was nothing to overshadow it. Then the villagers looked down upon the poor often-hungry tribes of hunters-and-foragers who wandered on the steppe or in the forest, and the villagers thought themselves very clever lads indeed, great breakers of tradition, sharp fellows liking new gadgets, go-ahead believers in progress who were always ready to scrap the old in favor of the new. I believe all this not only from theory, but from what actually happened. For in those villages there was no settling down, peasant-fashion, into hidebound conservatism. Instead, things raced on.

About this time I learned the trick of using sharpened stone, instead of merely sharp stone. From this discovery, indeed, the whole period is called the Neolithic, or New Stone Age, although the trick of how to sharpen or polish stone was not nearly as important as some others of that time. Yet it too had many values besides making the tool look prettier. Stones like flint and obsidian, which could be chipped into sharp points and edges, were brittle; they flew to pieces treacherously when you struck hard with them. But after I had learned to rub one stone against another until its edge slowly became sharp, then I could use heavier and tougher and more trustworthy stones. And at the same time of course I did not forget how to flake off a bit of flint or obsidian when I wanted a keener edge.

With sharpened stone I got for the first time a dependable ax, one behind which I could really put some muscle without always being afraid that the head would fly to splinters when it struck. A good ax was valuable to me at this stage for clearing back brush and trees and thus extending my new grain fields. A pioneer farmer must often live by his ax as much as by his hoe.

At the same time, with a better ax, I got better control over wood and a new skill at woodworking. Now more than before, I came to know the comfort of staunch oak, and the beauty of straight-grained pine, the tough lightness of ash, and the clean fragrance of new-hewn cedar.

Another great series of discoveries involved the whole process of carrying and storing. Foragers must have made a beginning here, because they had need to carry more nuts or acorns than they could hold in the hands, and because such foods would keep well. But when I became a farmer, both carrying and storing became more important, and I developed many ways of doing both, besides making use of natural containers like gourds.

First of all, a skin might be gathered up by the corners to make a kind of bag. Later it was fastened together into a real bag. It turned out to be a wonderfully useful device, and would even hold water. A bag had its shortcomings, such as not being able to hold its mouth open for filling. But in spite of all my later ingenuity I have never yet been able to replace it. Although I now make few of them out of hides, I still use millions of quite simple bags every year to transport and keep everything from water to coal and gold.

While I was working out the finished bag, I had probably, first perhaps in play, been exercising my nervous fingers in weaving rushes and withes into mats. A mat may be picked up at the corners like a hide. Then, when I had learned the trick of actually securing or weaving my mat into that shape, I had a basket. In its own way a basket was like a bag, an ideal container—light, durable, and handy. It kept its shape when empty and was easy to fill. To this day also I have not much improved upon it, and I still use millions of baskets which do not differ much from primitive ones and are even made of the same materials. Some tribes actually learned to weave their baskets fine enough to hold water. But, like the bag, the basket had its shortcomings; it was not really a good water-container, and it did not stand fire.

To overcome these two difficulties I must have begun to smear clay on the outside to keep the basket from scorching when it stood near the fire, and to smear clay on the inside so that it would hold water. As soon as such a basket had been accidentally burned in the fire, I saw that the clay turned reddish and became hard, like stone. By that time I was bright enough, and was sensitive to the ways of cause-and-effect. I seized the new idea, and began to make pots. At first, in making them, I imitated the natural shapes and even the textures of baskets, but after a while I learned to fashion them in an almost infinite variety of shapes, and to decorate them with designs and pictures in colors. Although the bag and basket were earlier, the pot seems to have come after the beginning of food-production, and it became a typical implement of the villagers.

Like the two others, the pot had its own advantages and shortcomings. Even from the first it held water fairly well, and after I had learned about glazes, it became a perfect container for any liquid. Also, it stood fire. The pot, however, was breakable, and heavy to carry. But again, I still use many millions of pots and dishes which do not differ essentially from the early ones.

The pot also was important in two subtler ways. It was the first of my manufactures which depended (even though I did not yet know it) upon direct chemical change. I may have begun to watch what fire did to other things besides clay, and eventually any such interest would lead to a great deal. Also, pottery gave my individuals a new means of self-expression, because formless clay so easily took and preserved any shape into which they wished to fashion it.

The importance of these carrying and storing devices was very great, for the growth of cities was to depend upon them. Large numbers of people could live at one place only when grain produced elsewhere in the growing-season was carried there, and stored, and used through the seasons when no crops were being grown.

Also the bag, the basket, and the pot form a good series to show the way in which later discoveries often do not replace earlier ones, but are merely added to them.

Another great discovery of this greatest of creative ages was the weaving of cloth. During many centuries already my hunters had worn the skins of animals, and with needle and thread they (or the wives and mothers) had sewn them into clothing. Skins were excellent in cold weather, but at times I wanted protection against the sun. Besides, I had long since developed the idea of modesty, so that in warm countries I wanted to cover my body without smothering myself under a sheepskin. Thus the first cloth to be known has been discovered in warm countries.

The suggestion could easily come from the weaving of mats and baskets, and actually the earliest cloth was produced by mere plaiting. Goat hair was perhaps the first material, because it could be woven into a thin and light fabric. Next—but this would probably have been long after agriculture was practiced—some clever fellows worked out the complicated process of growing, preparing, and weaving flax into linen. Later still, apparently, came the use of wool.

Thus gradually I, Man, developed the whole complicated and tedious process of textile manufacture in all its many details—shearing, breaking, combing and carding, washing, spinning, weaving, bleaching, dyeing, and only a cloth-maker knows what else.

Before long, cloth-making led my villagers to develop the loom, which was by far the most complicated machine which I had made so far. Nevertheless, it did not call for such a stroke of genius as did the invention of the bow, for most of its details could be worked out one at a time.

If there is anything which I have learned about life, as I look backward, it is that change seems to breed change. Nowhere do I see this better than in this same amazing period. Even by historical standards it cannot have been inordinately long; two thousand years might cover it. And though to food-production itself I have added sharpened stone, containers, and weaving, I have still hardly begun to tell of all the changes.

Agriculture developed in all directions. Millet may have been grown as early as any wheat or barley, and rice followed not so long after.

By now having learned many tricks, I captured some wild ducks, penned them up or cut their wings, fed them on my extra grain, and in a few generations had a breed of fat and complaisant tame ducks. Far in India, the jungle-fowls proved to be like dogs and pigs; they came scavenging, as their old name "dung-hill fowl" still seems to show. I then had at my service that stupid but useful creature the hen, and her handsome but equally stupid mate, the cock.

Once I had started to store grains, I began my not-yet-ended war with rats and mice. So, in spite of my ancient fear of the leopard, I welcomed the small cats which came prowling around the granaries. Some think, however, that I tamed the cat because of a religious belief. Since the ancient Egyptians were the first people known to have kept cats and since they held cats to be sacred and built temples for them, their domestication may indeed be an example of the working of a religious idea. But though there have also been sacred cows and dog-headed gods, I have less reason to think that the other animals were first tamed to placate the Other-world.

Another curious thing that I have noted is that anything new may have secondary results or by-products, not at all suspected at the beginning but in the end proving very useful. Sometimes indeed the secondary and unforeseen results have been the more important.

One thing, for instance, that no one may have suspected at the beginning was that the raising of crops and the keeping of animals would come together in natural alliance. In fact, anyone might even have thought just the contrary, and probably there were feuds between the keepers of flocks and the growers of grain. But soon my villagers learned that the two worked together like hand and foot. First of all, they supplied a healthful and pleasing variety of food. Also, I undoubtedly saw before long (although out of laziness I often did not put the learning to use) that manure aided the growth of plants. Then, on the other hand, my extra grain enabled me to feed animals and make them dependent upon me, and to fatten them.

As another unexpected result, consider all that developed from straw. Grains were grown primarily for the seeds, but the villagers also found themselves with large supplies of straw, and it proved to be useful in many ways. It was fodder for some animals, it caused the fire to blaze up quickly, it could be woven into mats and hats, it made good bedding for man or beast.

So things went with the animals too. Primarily most of them were tamed for a food-supply, and for such by-products as even hunters used—hide, bone, horn, and hair. The use of milk came afterwards. Probably, even in the older days, a hungry child sometimes suckled with the puppies at the dugs of a bitch, when famine lay heavy upon the tribe. (So may have begun those stories of Romulus and the other wolf-children.) As far as I know, no one ever made a practice of milking bitches or sows, but from very early times, some tribespeople milked ewes, she-goats, and cows. Later on, when the other animals were tamed, they milked she-asses, mares, she-camels, in fact almost every mammal big enough to be worth that trouble. Then from milk itself came all the other unsuspected and valuable products, such as curds, butter, cheese, and eventually casein-paints, glues, and plastics.

As for fowls, they were probably prized from the beginning, not only for the flesh and eggs, but also for their fine feathers. In fact, some tribes have kept fowls without eating either them or their eggs, merely to have their feathers to use for ornaments.

The special development of the sheep was the most surprising of all. The original wild sheep merely had hair much like a goat's, as the wild sheep still has. But after they had been under my protection the short fuzzy under-coat of certain individual sheep began (probably by a natural variation) to grow longer. In wild life such sheep might have been hindered in their movements and so might have been killed off as lambs without passing on this tendency to any lambs of their own. But perhaps this same growth made such sheep less active and less confident in themselves, so that they kept closer to the shepherd. Thus under the new conditions they had actually a better chance to survive. The shepherd also may have noted that these sheep were more docile, and so have spared their lambs. Perhaps they even amused him as curiosities. Soon also he found the skins of these sheep to make warmer cloaks.

In one way and another woolly sheep became desirable, and I must already have learned such simple facts as that a long-fleeced ram and a long fleeced ewe were likely to produce a long-fleeced lamb. So I probably urged nature along by saving the longest-fleeced for breeding. Thus, besides mutton, I came to have wool. And thus also, by the very opening of history, the sheep with its ridiculous fleece had become completely dependent upon me for protection, and was already a symbol of helplessness, mass-stupidity, and cowardice—in short, the most wholly domesticated of the animals.

Another secondary result sprang from my greater dependence on grain and from the making of pots. When I began to live largely on grain, I no longer merely chewed it with my teeth, but made special grinding-stones, which developed later into querns, metates, and hand-mills. I learned to mix the flour with water, perhaps first puddling them together on a flat stone, as a child mixes mud-pies. Then I poured the batter upon a well-heated stone, and baked a thin cake. But any great development of this making of batter, and of baking, had to wait for the pot, which had begun as a simple container before it became useful as a mixing bowl.

In another way too the pot revolutionized cookery. This was not just a matter of adding another frill to life by tickling the palate in new ways. (Even this, however, is not to be despised, for I know of nothing that has added more to the pleasure of my individuals than good cookery and tasty meals.) Fundamentally, the pot let me add boiling to the ancient roasting and broiling, and to the more recent baking. Once I could boil, I added a whole list to my victuals. The toughest meat grew softer after long boiling, and in time of famine even the bones yielded a little broth. Obviously all the tasty and nutritious soups had to wait upon the perfection of the pot. Moreover, such seeds as beans were not satisfactory even when cooked as a batter, and their use as a principal food of many peoples must have come after they could be cooked in a pot.

Cookery in fact gives me some clue to the time when I began to eat certain foods. Wheat, for instance, can be boiled, but is usually ground and baked; but rice, which can be ground, is usually boiled. It would be a good guess then that I established my habits with wheat before I had pots, with rice afterwards.

By and large, I really got too enthusiastic, and began to cook the life out of many vegetables, and even fruits, which were better eaten raw. But here again I was behaving in a very human way, for I have always noticed my difficulty of knowing when I had enough of a good thing.

Life was rapidly getting more and more complicated. And as the best symbol of complication I propose the fence. Hunters built fences only for game traps and for protection. Herdsmen often built no fences at all, and also a purely grain-growing people needed none, except perhaps around the edges to keep off wild animals. But once I had arrived at all the complications of village life, the problem arose.

At first the herds were watched during the days and thus kept from the fields. But they were usually penned at night, and this in itself was a start of fencing. So began that elaborate system (which now extends for millions of miles) of fences, walls, hedges, ditches, dikes, and what-not, that a community erects, not so much to protect itself against the outside as to keep its own quarreling elements apart.

15

I live in villages

Again I should like to look around—this time at the world of the millennium between 6000 and 5000 B. C. Already it is less easy to describe, because things have grown more complicated.

Most important were the villages where the people lived by raising crops and keeping animals. Perhaps some people raised crops without yet having learned to keep animals. On the other hand, there were probably some who raised no crops but lived the life of nomads, keeping goats and sheep. Possibly others lived by keeping herds of cattle, but I think this less likely. In any case, the nomads of this time cannot have been of much importance, for without horses and camels they lacked that swiftness and ease of movement which made possible the lordly nomads of a later time.

Beyond the lands of crop-grower and shepherd still ranged the tribespeople—few but hardy—who lived the old hunting-and-foraging life. And in jungle and along desert-margin, even yet perhaps lived some simple ones who wandered naked and ate their food where they found it, and by night crouched in rock-crannies and listened for the prowling leopard.

But those who lived in the villages were in the forefront, and through them my story runs on to the future. Those villages were small, but well enough built with houses. In them my people lived close to their animals, but yet probably with much security and decency, self-respect and happiness. Remember again that these were not the villages of three thousand years later, or of modern times, when the villagers had been for so many generations ground down by tyranny and taxation. As yet there was little problem of crowding, for by the new methods of production the food-supply easily increased as rapidly as the people. Perhaps already they said some version of that most hopeful of proverbs: "With every new mouth, God sends a pair of hands to feed it." In the villages even young children were useful, as they had never been among hunters. By six a boy was out helping watch the goats, and a little girl could hardly remember when she stopped making pots in play and began making real ones.

At this time, I think, the idea of "work" may first have sprung up. These people no longer lived the adventurous life of the hunter; farming involved laborious and not always interesting chores at regular times—and that is work. Yet anyone growing crops for himself and his family in the fields of his own village was scarcely conscious of the labor as a hardship, and many a one from seeing the heads forming on his wheat felt as intense a satisfaction as hunter ever gained from the kill. At most, the labor was not overwhelming. The villagers had only to support themselves—not a multitude of city-dwellers. They were not caught in the web of having to produce excess food to be bartered for complicated tools beyond their own power of making, and to be paid in taxes to support a court, and civil service, and army, and priesthood. Fields, also, were still more plentiful than people to work them, so that there was no necessity of grubbing harder and harder to produce less and less. The growing of wheat and barley under such conditions demanded heavy labor only in spurts, and yielded so much food in proportion to the work that people depending on grain had time for other things: for care of animals, weaving, and anything else. During the growing-season or after harvest, the men probably had time still to go hunting.

So this period which saw the beginning of work may also have seen the beginning of leisure. In fact, the one almost implies the other. The hunter might not have known whether he was working or playing, but he spent long hours in the process of getting the food for mere existence. The villager worked at tasks which may even have been disagreeable to him, but he spent fewer hours in obtaining his basic food-supply. From the tremendous changes arising in this period I should say on second thought that it must have been less an age of work than an age of leisure. For, as I have said before, only when people are well fed and have time to sit around and talk and think do they get new ideas and then develop them into new inventions and ways of life.

As yet, however, there was little real wealth, or the troubles that go with it. I do not claim it as a golden age of peace, but when I dig up one of those first villages I generally find no defending walls or palisades, and the weapons are hunters' tools, not instruments of war. Conquest, like weaving, is a technique, and it had not yet been invented. Around the edges, the hunting-people still lived by rule of spear and bow, but the hunting-people were few in numbers, and any trouble they stirred up would have been little more than occasional robbery and murder. The nomads may have been stronger, but at most they were raiders, not conquerors as yet. There were, I presume, quarrels between different villages over a land-boundary, or a wandering cow, or a stolen girl—but these were more like brawls and squabbles than organized wars. Sometimes they might develop into feuds, but just as likely, among people who were losing the savagery of hunters, they would be patched up, come harvest-time.

Life still centered in the family, and the village itself was a larger family, tracing its ancestry back to some hero or demi-god. Its remains show that all the houses were more or less of the same size—which I take for good enough evidence that no chieftain or priest lorded it over the others. Yet the villagers were too close to the hardness of life and death to be impressed with any theory of absolute equality. Village life had no secrets, and villagers had few illusions about one another. It was well known that So-and-so was stupid (though a good worker in the fields) and that Such-and-such was lazy (though clever with cattle), and that Such-another ran away and hid in a pile of straw when it was rumored that the desert-men were attacking. On the contrary, the villagers would know that some among them stood out from the crowd. They looked to one of themselves as their chief, but he was still, as with hunters, the first among equals, and any two were better than any one.

The same, I think, might be said for the priest. Probably each villager knew the rites and rituals. One person of course would have to lead and officiate, and compose new hymns and prayers; on days of festivals he seemed very important. But the rest of the time he worked in the fields along with the others, and no one paid him much attention. Also, it is possible, these villagers were passing through an age of doubt and reason. What religion they inherited from their ancestors was the religion of hunting-tribes, which consisted chiefly of rites designed to increase the supply of game. The last thing any villager wanted, however, was a lot of deer eating up his grain or a herd of wild cattle breaking down fences and trampling crops, and luring his tame cows away. The great discoveries of the villagers also make me think them a people who were not bound fast by tight bonds of superstition, but were accustomed to think for themselves.

Although village life was more complicated than hunting-and-foraging, it did not call for the constant split-second team-work of the chase. A farmer could work more by himself and for himself. Working together was necessary for defense, and for harvest, clearing of new fields, and digging of irrigation ditches.

Villagers might thus be even more democratic and individual than hunters, and they had not as yet specialized enough in their kinds of work to start breaking down their equality. Every grown male was a farmer, and he was still, when need was, a warrior. He built his own house, and made his own hoes and spears. Just as the chieftain or priest was a kind of spare-time chieftain or priest, thus also it went with the other trades. Anyone might go hunting, but doubtless some liked to go hunting better than others, and had more skill at it. They might pass their extra meat around to the others when they returned. Probably they did not actually think of bartering it for something else, but they naturally expected the others to share in their turns, as a matter of decency and honor. So also every villager could make a bow, but one might have more skill than the rest. He could make bows for the others, or more likely the others would first do the rough work and bring the half-finished bows to him for final shaping and polishing. So also it may have been with fishing, and building houses. But each of them was able to do, and often did, everything which needed doing; he was hunter, fisherman, carpenter, or bowyer, only upon an amateur basis.

The real separation of work was according to the three ancient classes of fathers, mothers, and children. The fathers kept their traditional duties of leadership, priesthood, fighting, hunting and fishing, and the making of tools and weapons. Of newer occupations they took over wood-working, building, and the care of the larger animals.

The mothers also kept their traditional duties: care of children and home, and cooking. But they needed to do little foraging any more, except to gather dainties like mushrooms, and herbs for flavoring and medicine. Of the newer occupations, butter- and cheese-making fell to the mothers along with the other preparation of food. They made the pots. With quick-flying hands and fingers they performed the endlessly repeated motions of spinning and weaving—a kind of work which a housewife did so easily that she gossiped or sang while she worked.

The children did their share by helping with household chores, by looking out for the gentler animals such as the milch goats, and by scaring the birds away from the crops. Besides, just as work was separating from leisure, so education was separating from play. A father, self-consciously, taught his son to sharpen a stone ax or recite the rituals; a mother schooled her daughters in the craft of the distaff. Already there was so much to be learned that a child did not merely absorb it in the process of growing up.

Just how the work of the fields was done is a little doubtful. The first planting may have been the invention of the mothers. It developed from foraging rather than from hunting, and in primitive tribes it is still the mother's work. The chances are that the kitchen-garden with its beans and onions and melons remained in her care in the village also. But grain-growing, with all its tilling, sowing, harvesting, and threshing, called for more activity and power. Probably the whole village—children and all—turned out for harvest, and from very ancient times the records show the growing of wheat and barley to have been the work of the fathers.

Of what those villagers were like, one by one, I know a little. They were no longer half-apes, I am sure, but must have been remarkably like any people you would meet today. Some were tender-hearted and some were cruel—or, to put it better, each had a vein of tender-heartedness mingled with a vein of cruelty. Some were fat and talkative, and some were thin with dreams in their eyes. And even one may have been thin and talkative, and another fat with dreams in his eyes. They had their amusements and their pains, their ecstasies and their frustrations. In fact, for various reasons, they may have been much more like modern people than many who came in the centuries later.

Of their way of thinking, I know little, but I suspect that it was not much different from the modern way. By the help of language they had probably worked up to wider and more complicated abstractions, like *freedom* and *righteousness*. Such ideas, put into words and combined into a set of traditions, helped to hold a tribe together, then as later, and to give the people a sense of a common heritage of what they may already have called "spiritual things." Already, moreover, such abstractions were probably causing trouble. A visitor, even among people speaking the same language, may have been shocked to find that *righteousness* had different limits here than at home. Besides, *righteousness* nearly always shifted, depending upon whether you were dealing with your own people or outsiders. It might be wrong to cheat your own people, but right to cheat outsiders.

Of their art, something survives. Like their villages, it was simple. They shaped their pots and weapons with care and in good design, and often enriched them with ornament. They played musical instruments, and held dances. I suppose that they sang songs, and early songs are always poetry. Undoubtedly they told stories, and many of these must still linger as tales of trolls and bear-sons, of Samson the strong man, or of clever little Hermes, the thieving rogue. Another of their stories must be that of Cain and Abel, and from its plot I think it was one first told of a village hero and his killing of the rascally nomad Abel, whose herds had ravaged the grain fields. But later, as the story now runs, it was re-told by nomads so that Cain the wicked grain-grower brutally killed the innocent Abel. But even this twisting of a story to suit the needs of one people rather than of another has a modern tinge to it. Yes, compared with hunters-and-foragers these villagers seem just around the corner.

As more food was produced, there came to be more and more people, and they went out to plant more and more villages. These were not isolated one from the other, but individuals passed back and forth, exchanging things and ideas, and sharpening mind against mind, as they had learned to sharpen stone against stone.

So perhaps, when harvest was over, two young fellows took a goat-skin dressed in the way of their village, and walked across the mountain through the forest. They carried their bows, for there was always a chance of meeting the shifty hill-men or a bear. When they came to the other village, they told news and listened to it; they gossiped and ate the food that was given them; and as they ate, they stole glances at the girls. They learned that the new kind of wheat, brought up from the south as seed the last year, had yielded only a disappointing crop; they listened to a variety of explanations why, and added some of their own. One of them, seeing that the housewife was weaving at a rather old-fashioned loom, told how it might be improved just a trifle. They laughed over a new story (quite an indecent one), and told another in return. They learned of a rumor that far-off to the northeast the desert-men had raided. They gave the goat-skin to the villager who had been their host, and with all politeness he gave them in return a polished shell which had come from a village farther west. Then they went home—ambassadors, traders, and news-bearers—well fed, happy, thinking about the girls, and quite confident that the world was theirs for the taking, as is the right of young blades always in a prosperous democracy.

Something like this, life may have been in that little-short-of-magical millennium from 6000 to 5000 B. C. In some places, the new ways of life were just beginning, as emigrants from older villages cleared away thickets with their stone axes, or as hunting-tribes planted their first crops. In other places, the new way was already becoming old, and the fathers began to say, stolidly: "This is the way we do, because thus our great-grandfathers did, and so from the beginning—*there is no other*!"

But in other villages, they still said, as their great-grandfathers had: "This is the way to do because it has advantages, as any reasonable person can see—or at least we have not much to lose, and it is *worth the trying*."

16

Where? Who?

THUS far I have paid very little attention to which ones among my tribes or races may have accomplished this or that, or in what part of the world. Such matters do not interest me greatly; for I, Man, obviously include within myself all tribes, and this is my story. Still, the matter is not wholly without importance, and as concerns the origin of food-production, I can give what seems to me a good enough answer.

All the evidence points to a rather small region. It begins with the valley of the lower Nile in Egypt, swings into Asia through Palestine, Syria, and the Mesopotamian lands along the Euphrates and Tigris, and then leads on across the broad Iranian plateau into the valley of the Indus. Along this strip were to be found in a wild state all the plants and animals upon which the great discoveries were based. Also, all the evidence of archeology points to an origin somewhere in this region.

From east to west this is a stretch of something over two thousand miles; from north to south of about five hundred. Yet, compared with the whole earth—which is my home—it is small. Since I am no more concerned with Egypt than with Mesopotamia or any other country, I have no special interest in that endless argument as to which came first, and certainly my present state of knowledge does not make a final decision possible. Possibly some further diggings will prove that the great revolution, or this and that phase of it, originated outside of this area; more likely they will narrow the limits more closely inside of it. But that decision lies in the future, and is a small matter after all.

As for the people, I believe that they were neither black nor yellow, and also that they were not pink and fair-haired. In all likelihood they were black-haired and brunette. Often, especially when tanned by the sun, they appeared brown of skin, but their thin lips and straight or curly hair made them of the "white" race. They were neither tall tropical blacks nor big-sinewed northern blonds; instead, most of them were small and rather delicately built.

Many of their descendants are presumably living in that same region today. Still, I cannot advise any particular nation to puff itself up with ancestral pride. The original discoveries were very likely made by small tribes which may since have lost their identity completely, and I think it a better than even chance that the Egyptians and Mesopotamians borrowed the tricks of food-production from some other peoples, just as a few thousand years later the Europeans took over civilization from the Egyptians and Mesopotamians.

The next natural question, however, may well be, "Why did these people, rather than some others, make these great discoveries?" I am unable to see how their skin-color or hair-type could have helped them, but I see a possible significance in the small body. Any individual who lacks physical power is likely to start using his brain more, and I suppose the same might be true for a race, which after all is only a multiplication of individuals. But, even so, I can scarcely do more than ask the question: "Did these people make their great discoveries because they were particularly talented as a race?" Or, to shift ground slightly, "Was it because they produced a rather large number of highly talented individuals?" I do not know, and probably can never know.

For one thing, the question always gets mixed up with another one, for there is the problem of land as well as of people. So I can ask: "Did these people live in a kind of country which led them on to achievement, at a time when other races lived in less favorable countries?"

Since the whole stretch from the Nile to the Indus had much in common, any believer in the importance of land and the unimportance of people can put up a good argument. All that country was part of the hot and dry belt which lies just outside of the tropics. It was a naturally healthful region, where people were neither plagued by tropical parasites nor constantly afflicted with colds and pneumonia, as they were in the North. But the most favorable feature of the land, I think, was its variety of hot dry plains and cool well-watered mountains. At the bottom, so to speak, lay the flat deltas, the valleys of the great rivers, and the salt-flats of the desert sinks. But almost everywhere you saw high mountains on the horizon.

As you walked toward those mountains, this was the way the land changed. First lay the broad stretch of plain sparsely covered by desert-scrub, with wild-asses raising the dust as they scurried off. Then you came to the grass-lands of the benches and foothills, and some of the grass might be wild barley. Next you entered brush-country, and perhaps a wild bull stood louring at the edge of a thicket, and pawed the earth. You saw more cattle higher up, in the parkland where the country grew beautiful with copse, grove, and meadow. Now there were patches of wild wheat in the meadows, torn sod where wild pigs had rooted beneath the oaks, flowing streams of clear water, and trout rising. Afterwards, the wind sucked down-valley with a chill in it, and you came to pines and tall cedars. Still farther, the climbing grew steeper, and the forest thinned, and at last you looked on and sharply upwards, seeing mountain slopes of green grass broken by crags, where wild sheep and wild goats fed, and still higher the silent whiteness of the great peak—awesome, like the Other-world.

That was not a journey usually to be taken in one day —but neither, in most parts of that country, would it take a month. The point I would make, however, is that on the slopes of such a mountain-range a tribe could find healthful and pleasant country having all the necessary plants and animals along with good water, stone for tools, and all sorts of wood for fuel, bows, hafts, and houses. It was also a country in which hunters would naturally have lived, to begin with. It offered the greatest variety, and the stimulation to the mind which springs from the challenge of change. By walking twenty miles up or down the slope one achieved the range of a thousand miles north and south.

In some mountain valley I would look for the beginnings of my great discoveries. Even yet that is the kind of country which I hold beautiful, and I gladly return to it from plain and city. I notice also that for the simple life a various country is better. When the Americans were going west, they often settled on poorer land in the mountains or at the edge of prairies because there they found wood, water, and game; but later they took up the lands of richer soil but more lacking in other supplies. There is also another detail of evidence—that the people in many of the early cities of the river-plains raised artificial hills for their temples, thus showing probably that in their past they had lived among real hills.

I should like to know, but probably shall never learn, whether all the great discoveries sprang from one center, or whether one originated in one place and another in another, or whether the same discovery occurred in more than one place. I see some argument for this last when I consider the pig, which is different in different regions, and in each is derived from the wild swine of that country, even as far off as China. Thus it would seem that different peoples may have domesticated the pig independently. But this is far from certain. For one thing, pigs are not easily driven long distances, especially across dry country, and so a traveling tribe could take along the idea and the memory much more easily than the actual animals. Then they would find little difficulty in taming the wild pigs of their new country.

In general, as most people will agree, invention is more

difficult than borrowing. Just as all the telephones in the modern world trace back to one inventor, so all the pots in the world, ancient and modern, may trace back to one inventor. But of course I am not sure.

There is certainly no reason, however, why the same people who invented pottery should also invent weaving. On the whole, since so many discoveries came so quickly, I think that many tribes contributed and that ideas were passed in all directions. But as yet I can only be even reasonably sure in a few minor details, such as, that hens came from India, and that cats were domesticated in Egypt. The early Egyptians indeed seem to have had a real knack with animals, and even made a beginning of domesticating gazelles and baboons.

At least this is certain—the villagers, in one place and another, established a very successful way of life, so that they increased in numbers and had to go out and establish more and more villages. Eventually, even if not at the beginning, villages sprang up on the wide and rich river-valleys and became more numerous there than elsewhere, because of the rich soil. Before long, a dozen of them might lie within easy walking-distance, and through these villages—not through those more isolated ones among the hills and mountains—the main thread of my story runs on.

17

I learn about power

FROM the very beginning, whenever I wanted to go anywhere or do anything, my source of power had been my own body. I had perfected various instruments, such as the bow, for the transformation of this power. From very early times, also, I had used a stick to pry with, and from it had learned the principle of the lever. But—bow, lever, and everything else—the source of the power was the straining of my own muscles. Only at a rather late period did I catch at that other trick of how to make use of new sources of power for my own ends. This discovery was hardly second even to food-production in enabling me to gain control of the world, and before long also it changed the relation of one individual to another. Still more, it multiplied personal pleasure, for from that day to this there has been nothing which anyone has enjoyed doing more than lolling at his ease while hard work was being done for him. Like other discoveries, it had another side also; more and more a craving for power came to be, in many individuals, like a gnawing cancer, which they must feed until they died.

First, for the control of power, came the training of the power-animals. As I look back over the domestic animals I can see that first of all came the dog, whose duties are too many to be described in a word. Next, after many thousands of years, I got the food-animals. Then at last I learned how to use the power-animals, of which the first were the ass and the draught-ox.

Before I take up this great achievement, however, I might point out its curious connection to something which had happened a long time before. This forms another fine example of the way in which something first developed for one end is later used for quite another. I refer here to the whole business of cords, ropes, and knot-tying.

Pliant withes and the sinews of animals were natural cords, but they could have been of little use until someone, twisting them around this way and that, discovered about tying a knot. After this trick proved useful, I could easily have cut hides into thin strips and thus got thongs. By twisting or plaiting two or three thongs together I had a stronger but yet pliant thong, which could be pieced together and thus become a rope of any length wanted. The same could be done with plant fibers. From the making of rope came, I think, the spinning of thread, for the larger is often easier than the smaller to conceive and work out.

The point is, however, that I learned to make ropes and tie knots. Having done so, I learned the useful and amazing properties of ropes. They were flexible and yet strong; they were easily fastened by tying; they transmitted pull but not push; they adjusted perfectly to all shifts in the direction of pull.

Then, out of ropes and knot-tying, someone developed a lasso. As an invention, it was almost as amazing as the bow, although not nearly so important. Ordinarily anyone would find it easier to kill a gazelle or deer by shooting an arrow into it from arrow-range rather than by lassoing it from roping-distance. The very difficulty, however, may have made the undertaking a sporting event; to capture an animal, subdue it, and bring it home uninjured, may have been a series of feats for anyone to attempt. On the famous Lion Hunt Palette, which is prehistoric Egyptian, two of the hunters have lassos made of twisted rope and one of them has just roped a gazelle around the horns.

Now, to go back to the power-animals, you can see why ropes were important. First, such an animal was not like a pig, which needed never be caught except once—when it was to be butchered. A power-animal must be caught every time it was to be used, and a lasso was often the best means. Then, afterwards, if you put a pack or saddle on it, you had to have ropes for girths and lashings. Lastly, you might need more ropes or thongs for bridles, whips, tethers, tugs, reins, halters, and lead-ropes.

Dogs, sheep, and goats were too small to be worth the trouble, and saddling the pig has always been merely a funny idea. Doubtless the ox was tried, but the ox moved too slowly, and never seems to have been much used as a beast of burden. The first was probably the ass.

Wild asses were common along the Nile in village days, and a great deal points to their having been first domesticated there. Since I had by then gained much experience, the process was probably as wholly conscious as the development of the automobile—which does not mean, of course, that it was done without trial-and-error and much blundering. I should merely think that someone who was good with a lasso went out and roped a young ass. When it struggled in terror, he choked it into submission. He brought it to the village, kept it tied or penned, fed it well, got it used to him, doubtless with the help of a great deal of good and bad advice from the other villagers, he worked out some kind of panniers or pack-saddle, and eventually broke the ass to burden-bearing, with the help of many chokings and much beating. At last the ass settled down to carrying water-skins, or wood for the fires, or stones from the quarry in the hills to the village where they were shaped and used.

The mention of such kinds of work gives the best idea of why beasts of burden were used in later villages rather than in earlier ones. The earliest villages, in the hills or near the edge of the plains, could be close to all necessities. A villager needed to do little heavy carrying over long distances, and so he had small incentive to go to the trouble of training a wild ass. But when villagers thought principally of good soil, they might build far out on the plain or in some other spot where transportation became a problem worth solving.

Very likely it was not all so simple as this, but there is no reason to think that the training of an ass was a complicated problem. Nevertheless it was tremendously important. When the first one trotted along beneath his burden, doubtless his master was much pleased, but if any gray-bearded elders looked on, they may well have shaken their heads and said, "This is something never seen before. Who can say just what it may lead to?" They were right.

Before long there were pack-trains of asses trotting along the trails, and behind them the master throwing stones and beating them over the rumps, and yelling—as you can still see any day in Mexico and many other parts of the world. (All this—although I lack exact information—must have had much to do with the invention, or at least the great development of profanity.)

In this same general period, possibly even before the Egyptians trained the pack-ass, some of the Mesopotamian or Syrian people learned the use of draught-oxen. (First they may have discovered how to operate on their bull-calves so that they developed, not into dangerous bulls, but into easy-going oxen—in itself a symbolic mastery of power.)

While the ass was not very strong but could trot along as fast as his driver could go, the ox was exceedingly strong but very slow. The ass therefore was better as a pack-animal, but when I had once looped a rope around the horns of an ox (or even of a cow), and learned how much one of them could pull, I had an answer to the problem of great but slow-moving power. At first the thing to be moved might be any heavy object like a rock, or a tree-trunk to be used for a beam. Next I learned to attach the ox to a mud-sledge, and to make yokes.

Along with draught-oxen came also the plow, although possibly it was pulled by the villagers themselves before they learned about oxen. The plow in itself, although important, was just one more of the many inventions of this thriving period. Essentially the simplest plow was only a smallish tree cut off at the proper distance above the point where a large branch forked off. Then the trunk itself became the plow-beam, and the sharpened stub of the cut-off branch turned downward, became the plowshare to stir up the ground. The plow made a great difference in agriculture, and since it involved the use of large animals, plowing was always the fathers' work. Yet, in a period which was inventing so many things, I could take the plow in my stride.

The same, I think, can be said for the wheel, although people have been accustomed to grow eloquent about it, along with the plow. The wheel, however, was only a rather late development of the moving-part idea, and of that other basic and wonderful idea of rotary motion. Far back in the hunting-and-foraging time some idler perhaps moved his two palms back and forth upon a stick held between them, and noticed that the stick penetrated the mud or soft earth beneath it. Although the stick may have been roughly shaped, the hole was beautifully round. Whoever first noticed such a very strange fact had begun a phase of human development which was to lead on through the wheel and so to most of the complexities of modern machinery. Even before the Old Stone Age ended, the drill had been invented, and steady-handed workers had learned how to put little holes through bits of shell to make beads. Many of these holes seem to the eye to be just as good circles as a modern machine can drill. This discovery, like some others, was all the greater because the processes of nature drill few round holes. The pot-holes in a river-bed are about the only ones I can remember at the moment, and even these are seldom exactly circular.

Actually, however, the villagers had less use for carts and wagons than you might think at first. From earliest times they had used paths and trails, and even the passageways between their houses might be very narrow. Pack asses could squeeze between houses, and trot easily along paths, where carts could not go. A wheeled vehicle is no better than the road it travels, as most drivers of automobiles have realized at one time or another. So pack-animals, in the poorer parts of the world and especially among mountains, have always held their own against all the prowess of wheels.

The plow and the wheel were merely devices for putting the power of animals to work. These same villagers, however, some of whom lived along the large rivers, learned to tap a wholly different and new source of power.

From my earliest times I had known that strange thing, the wind. I could not see it, but I felt it, and saw its force in the lashing of branches and the swirling of dust. It was like my breath, which I felt against my hand—warm or cold—but could never see, except in momentary puffs on frosty days. In developing my ideas of the Other-world, I naturally mixed up wind, air, and breath with mind and soul, which also could not be seen, although in some way or other they seemed to be powerful.

During all those centuries the power of the wind had been chiefly a nuisance, blowing my hat off or lodging my grain. But the villagers, both along the Nile and the Euphrates, had long been accustomed to the use of boats, and depended largely upon fish. A fisherman could scarcely help noticing that his boat drifted with the wind, to his disadvantage as often as to his advantage. Eventually, however, he learned to make use of the wind, paddling with it when possible and mooring among the rushes when it was blowing too hard against him. Still later, having poles and mats and ropes all available, someone grasped the idea of a sail.

The trick of the first sailing was merely this: You put up the sail when the wind was with you, and so made a quick and easy run. But when the wind was against you, you put the sail down and paddled—at least being no worse off than you were without a sail. But in many places the wind blew one way in the morning and the other way in the evening. Thus, by choosing the time, you sailed both ways. Many centuries elapsed before anyone solved the problem of sailing against the wind—and no wonder, for the very idea seemed impossible on the face of it!

The rope, incidentally, was as much involved with wind-power as with animal-power. Even in a simple sailing-boat some ropes were useful, and before things had run their full course these ropes multiplied into stays, bunt-lines, foot-ropes, log-lines, halyards, vangs, painters, shrouds, hawsers, mizzen-topgallant-braces, spanker-boom-topping-lifts—and dozens more that only Captain Horatio Hornblower could name.

Thus, by the aid of the simple but marvelous rope and the tying of it into knots, while I was still living in villages, I had solved the problem of power as applied to transportation, and so successfully that no basic change was made until after 1800 A. D.

This solution, like food-production, was two-horned. On land, I used animals; on water, the wind. Curiously enough, I never mastered the use of wind for transportation on land, or the use of animals for transportation on water, although the former has often intrigued my imagination, and although the latter would have been practical enough for river-boats by means of tread-mills and paddle-wheels.

18

Power in earth and fire

BY THIS time, with the use of power-animals, I should say that I was definitely leaving the simple village behind, and entering into the period of the highly developed village, which was rapidly passing over into something still different. The trouble with those villagers, as some would think, was that they never let well-enough alone. Before they had got one change well established, they were off to add something else to it. And, as a conservative-minded person can aptly say at this point, a lot of trouble they got themselves into by such goings-on!

About this time—that is, around 4000 B. C.—some of these villagers began to learn much more about metal-working. In many books my development has been divided into the Old Stone and New Stone Ages, then the Ages of Copper, Bronze, and Iron. This is a natural enough division when implements are the chief means of classifying, but just as the New Stone Age involved more important matters than the polishing of stone tools, so also the discovery of how to work metal was only one of many important discoveries of this still creative age when the villages were rapidly growing more complicated.

Metal-working sprang up naturally and properly along with the new discoveries of power, for in all succeeding ages a concentration of power has demanded metal, as in an axle or dynamo. Also wealth was best expressed by collections of metal, and wealth soon came to be power in another sense. Thus from a very early time the symbols of power became, and have remained—gold, iron, and steel. "Who holds metal, he holds power."

First of all, and even far back before the time of villages, I saw the shining yellow bits of strange stone in the dull sand of a stream-bed, and picked out some of the bigger chunks because of their color and glitter. I treasured the yellow nuggets because they were rare and pretty, and I wore them for ornament, like other pretty stones and shells. After a while I came to think of such things as having power of magic. (Perhaps their charm was, not only that they were beautiful, but also that they were immortal. Already I knew how quickly beauty passed. The flower and the sunset wilted and paled as I watched them, and the beauty of a loved face faded almost as soon. But shining stone outlived the wearer, and still glowed as bravely as ever.)

At first the yellow stuff merely fell within the circle marked off by my word *stone*, for I found it among stones, and it was heavy, chunky, and hard. It was not all of the same color, but ranged from reddish through yellow to whitish. I found other stones like it, but less shining. Some were greenish or purplish, but when scraped or hammered showed a fine red. Others were black. These last I called *thunderstones* or *stones from heaven*, because I sometimes saw them fall from the sky; naturally I stood in awe of them, and even set some of them up to be worshipped.

The yellow stones were small, but now and then I came upon a red or black chunk which was of good size and shape for an ax-head. This was a great find! The next easy step was to realize that the red stone could be gradually pounded with a stone-hammer into the shape of an ax-head or even of a knife. Then I really had a copper knife, but my means of making it were still those of the Stone Age.

The next step probably came after I had learned what a strange effect fire had in turning soft yellow clay into hard red pottery. Perhaps this "miracle," as anyone might well have thought it, encouraged pot-makers to throw different kinds of earth and stone into the hot fire, just to see what happened.

Or, by accident, some people built a hot fire among certain black stones. After it cooled, they noticed some red beads which stood out on the surfaces. I can almost hear the argument:

"They were there all the time; we just didn't notice them before."

"This is the work of spirits! I want nothing more to do with it."

"Maybe the red beads were inside the stone, and the fire burned off the outside."

"But if fire makes clay into pottery, why can't it change some kinds of stone also?"

At last, on some occasion, the true explanation of the

unafraid and clear-thinking ones had to be accepted, because they tried it again and made it work.

Thus with copper, which stands as the type of the first metal, I passed through much the same progress as with food. First, I hunted for it and picked it up, as I had gathered wild wheat. Later, I learned to make beads of copper sprout from certain kinds of rock, much as wheat sprouted from the ground. In neither case could I actually produce something from nothing. But just as cultivation made wheat more plentiful, so I discovered that copper was not nearly so rare as it seemed, but could be produced rather plentifully from its ores.

By now I had become fully aware of the value of copper; it combined the weight and sharpness of stone with the toughness of wood, and had also its own qualities of being beautiful, and workable by pounding. Having learned so much, I would have been stupid indeed not to try many different kinds of earth and stone, and to build hotter and hotter fires in trying to get metal out of them. Undoubtedly I got many strange results, perhaps got something once, and then had to wait a long time before I could get it again, and then try still and fail many more times before I learned to control conditions properly and do it regularly. I found that I never got the yellow metal or the thunder-stone by means of fire. But, when trying for the red one, I sometimes got a white and shining one, and another which was dull and gray and heavy and soft, and still another one which was dark brown and very hard. Or there might be many shadings in between. (From these same trials, I also learned to make glass, which was almost as beautiful as gold, and in the long run almost as useful as copper.)

At last I knew that I was dealing not with one metal or with a great many, but with a few which ran together into an indefinite number of minglings.

It was all very difficult. The kinds were not set off sharply, like grains. I knew wheat and I knew barley, and there was no gradation of wheat-barley, and barley-wheat between them. But I found every shading between the white of silver and the yellow of gold. Sometimes when my furnaces cooled down, I got the red of copper, and sometimes the brown of bronze. It was hit-or-miss, and I did not master the problem for a long time.

Even though I could produce copper, I still knew little about it. From the bottom of my furnace or smelting-pit, I merely picked up whatever irregular chunks of metal I could find. Probably I did not realize that it had run there in liquid form, or else I saw no importance that it had.

But as long as I merely took this copper and pounded it into shape, I had not grasped the real secret of working it. That trick may have developed by help of that dull heavy kind of metal which I got from certain ores. It was neither beautiful nor did it have much practical use. But of all the commoner metals, lead was the only one to melt in a moderately hot fire. A fire hot enough to melt copper usually had to be built up in some kind of furnace, or even if it was in the open, its heat kept me too far away to notice just what happened. But without difficulty I could actually see a lump of lead lose shape and run, like wax. When it hardened again, it remained in the shape of whatever hollow in the ashes it had happened to run into. This was a quality which I had already seen with wax and fat.

Possibly native copper had been melted before the discovery of ore-smelting. More likely, I think, lead gave the hint. I made hot and clean fires by using charcoal and blowing with a bellows and building furnaces with flues. Then the crude copper from the smelting-pit melted again, and gold and silver also flowed like water.

Having melted them—all except iron—I learned to run the liquid metal into molds shaped in clay or cut in stone. When they cooled, the metals held the shape I wished. Silver and gold remained too rare for anything but ornaments. Copper also was still rare enough for the casting of many copper bracelets, but also I learned to run it into the form of a knife or spear-point or ax-head.

These were weapons. It was worth the cost, to labor hard or pay much for a weapon. If the stone hoe struck a stone and broke, that was a nuisance, but you made a new hoe. If the obsidian dagger splintered on the shield-rim, you were left with an empty hand and panic in the heart, as the copper knife rose up and fell flashing redly in the sun. "Yes, my child, good weapons are a comfort to the heart and the cost not to be counted, though the belly goes hungry. And so it was, even in the time of my grandfather."

In a way, the spectacular discovery of metal-working failed to accomplish very much at the time. Metal did not give me power over the animals, for I had that already. It did not give me power over the fields, for I was getting along well enough with hoes of stone and plows of wood. Eventually metal was to give me great new power over the world, but for thousands of years its chief use was for weapons with which one individual sought to kill another—a kind of struggle in which I, Man, who always embrace both parties, am not usually much interested.

In another way also the discovery of metal-working seems a lost opportunity. The whole process was really a course in chemistry and physics. Stimulated by new discoveries, some group of individuals might have set my development several thousand years ahead, if they could only have seen some universal quality in what they were doing, if they could only have carried on some theoretical experiments instead of working only for practical ends, if they could only have grasped the abstract instead of the concrete problem. But if anyone has been on the earth as long as I have, he looks back upon too many lost opportunities to worry much about any one of them.

19

More power—another kind!

BY THAT time, when I had trained the pack-ass and draught-ox and had established metal-working, the center of my still-rapid advance had definitely become the highly developed villages which clustered thickly in broad valleys and deltas.

Such low country, swampy in places and often overflowed, may seem quite unlovely, but for a villager it was very attractive. Primarily he liked it for its rich soil, which under the hot and unclouded sun brought out magnificent crops of wheat and barley. The grazing was not so good for sheep as on the uplands, but cattle did well, and pigs and ducks were at home. Fish were always plentiful; water-fowl were easy to kill in their seasons. Land could be reclaimed from the swamps by the digging of drainage ditches and the piling up of little dikes; by the opposite method fields could be extended into the desert-margins by the digging of irrigation canals. Either way of doing probably involved less work than the clearing of forest.

Actually, some of the villages were built upon a support of woven reed-mats to keep them from settling into the mud. The creation-story of *Genesis* probably originated among the Sumerians, who lived in the delta of the Euphrates, and you can notice that the very first act in creating the earth was to separate the water from the dry land. Such an idea originated easily among swamp-dwellers.

Nevertheless, those low valleys and deltas hemmed in by sea and desert were not like some lush tropical islands where people live comfortably without much thinking or working. The weaving of a mat to support a village, for instance, called for ingenuity, industry, and much work-together spirit.

By the new methods of production, food was plentiful, and the climate was healthful enough. There came to be more people. Again and again a village grew so large that its fields stretched off too far. When it took an hour or more to walk from the village to the outer fields, the time and effort became too great. Then some of the families moved to the edge of the fields, four or five miles away, and built a new village. They kept a sentimental tie with the older village where their kinsfolk still lived; they went back to it for religious festivals; and between old village and new there was taking and giving in marriage.

At the same time life was always, and not so slowly, getting more and more complex. There were new crops and new methods of growing them to be learned, and more and more new tricks about the breeding and tending and training and using of animals. Farming was becoming so complicated that anyone had all he could do just to be a farmer, without going in for building his own house and fashioning his own tools. Even when hoes were still made of stone, they were sometimes the work of professional tool-makers, as their standardized form and finish still show.

So it also went with the other crafts. After the invention of the potter's wheel, pottery passed into the hands of special craftsmen. From its very beginning, metalwork was out of the range of the ordinary farmer, and the smith arose as something new in the world. The farmer then had to produce enough extra food to barter for tools and pots. Since he thus saved a great deal of time, he was better off; the potter and the smith undoubtedly preferred their special work to the labor of the fields, and so they too were better off. Any village philosopher must have decided that it was all working for the best in the best of all possible worlds.

Just as individuals were tending to become specialists, so also it must have been happening with whole villages. The basis of life was grain. If a certain region was especially good for grain, people settled there. Yet the very qualities making lands excellent for grain-growing made them unfit to support the village in other ways. Stones were essential for hoes, but there were no stones in the rich silt. The only wood to be found was poor, or there might be no trees at all. Grain-growing did not fit in well with pasturage. And anyone could look till his eyes burst out before finding copper-ore in a delta.

Villagers in such a location had to take time off to go and get flints, wood, and other supplies. But soon it would work out that only certain ones went to get the supplies, and thus they became merchants, trading flint and wood for barley and wheat. I do not know when anyone first said, "Travel is broadening," but it must have been true from the first, and also there is nothing like trading and bartering with foreigners to sharpen the wits and keep the mind open to new ideas.

Looking over a whole region I can see that there were coming to be different kinds of villages. Along the edge were those where the people were mostly shepherds. Other villages grew large crops of grain, and traded the surplus for sheep and what else they needed. Still another village which was on a river depended a good deal on fish, and traded some dried fish for other things. Again the village philosopher must have decided that it was all working for the best.

At this point I can conceive of two outcomes, since the situation was not likely to remain in perfect balance. I can imagine, first, that the farmers might have remained more important as owners of land, keeping the smiths, potters, merchants and all the other new kinds of workers as servants and inferiors. Or, second, the farmers might have sunk into industrious but stupid fellows, who got little for their hard work.

Actually, it came about in the latter way. The greater complexities of life worked to the farmer's disadvantage. For example, the building of larger irrigation works put him under the power of anyone who could control the flow of the water—perhaps miles away up-stream. The greater rewards began to go to people who were not laborers in the fields and nurse-maids to sheep and cattle.

And wherever the rewards were greater, there the cleverer youngsters flocked, as they have done since trees had leaves, and always will.

But where did they flock to? For, so far, I have not mentioned anything but slightly different kinds of villages. Something new, however, really was developing, and I can work out well enough, I think, how it was happening.

When, let us say, some individual first went in for making pots as a craft, he naturally made them at his own house. People of the village and of near-by villages came there to barter for them—two measures of barley, or a sheep-skin, or a young pig. In some other village, another individual developed skill at making stone-tools. But it was a nuisance for anyone to have to go to one village for a pot and clear away to another village for a stone-hoe. Soon, a tool-maker would set up his miniature factory-and-shop close to the potter, and a new potter got to work in the village where the tools were first made.

From these first simple craftsmen soon developed the trader and keeper of a shop. The potter took in barter more sheepskins than he and his family knew what to do with, and so he re-traded a sheep-skin for something else. Before long, his house was known as a place primarily to get a pot, but also you had a good chance of finding him ready to trade you a sheep-skin, or some dried figs, or a copper bracelet. Then his son, if he had no great knack at pottery, might turn into a kind of merchant or keeper of a trading-post.

Thus already certain villages were getting larger and

more complicated because the families of the potter and the tool-maker and the trader lived there. Very likely, also, those villages were rather large ones to begin with; they might well have been the mother-villages to which many people were already in the habit of returning for festivals. When they had also become, even in a small way, centers of manufacture and trade, you could just as well begin to use a new word, and call them—towns.

That is only one way, however, perhaps only part of one way, in which it might have happened. As the country grew more crowded with villages, troubles sprang up, which led to the growth of towns. When people moved out from their original centers founding new villages as they went, they kept their friendship with the people of the other villages which had originated from the same center. But they looked with at least some slight suspicion upon the villagers who had spread out from other centers. They may even have used some word like *foreigner* because those others had different (and somewhat shocking) customs, and spoke in a queer dialect.

When disputes arose, as disputes will, there was a brawl between the two boundary villages. The defeated ones ran to their comrade villages, showing their bruises and telling of foreign aggression and atrocities. Then both districts turned out in force, and the result was perhaps a fairly good imitation of a pitched battle, rather awkwardly fought with stones, and clubs and boar-spears, for by this time probably most of the villagers did not use bows. Such a scuffle would soon end in the rout of one side, with few killed on either side. Possession of the boundary field (or whatever was the cause of it all) was thus settled temporarily at least, and both sides went home with somewhat deeper suspicion of the other. Most of the individuals of both villages went back to farming with contentment, for in common opinion, that was the real way to live—not by fighting. But a few bigger-muscled and more quarrelsome fellows swaggered about with tales of their deeds in the battle, and took to making better weapons and practicing with them. Whoever had been the leader in the battle remained something of a head-chief afterwards, and added some prestige to whatever village he lived in.

A soldier-class sprang up in various other ways. When metal or wood or other goods had to be brought from a distance, the caravans were sometimes raided by the hunting- or nomad-peoples. The remedy was to have the valuable cargo escorted by some big, well-armed guardsmen. And how about the robbers themselves? They were good fellows to have on your side, for pay, on the day of battle. Then, also, the villagers who lived on the edges of the desert and mountain were used to continual skirmishing with the nomads, and thus never lost that love of fighting which was the natural heritage of hunters.

By this time the town was getting bigger, and there was a certain piling up of extra food in granaries and extra gadgets of all kinds in the houses of craftsmen and traders. The craftsmen and traders could pay for what they wanted. One thing they wanted was advice about the future and peace with the Other-world. So, even if he had not arisen already, the professional priest now began to be a very prosperous person.

Some think that the whole shift from village to town

was most closely connected with the piling up of extra goods. Whoever controlled these held a club, and could use it as he wished. Very often the priest—not at all the same kind of person as the part-time and rather harried village priest—was the one who got this control.

Thus during the centuries when I was domesticating the power-animals and mastering the power of metal, I was also learning tricks of power of another kind. A few people were coming into control, and were living more richly. At the same time the ordinary farmers were getting more numerous and having to work harder to raise enough food to support themselves and to barter for tools and pots and the services of soldiers and priests.

It looks a little like a sinister conspiracy of gangsters, but most likely it was nothing of the sort. It may have been a blind process of which no one was conscious at all. Or it could even have moved step by step with the leaders always acting from the best and highest and most self-sacrificing of motives. Seeing that the people were hungry, a priest planned a new irrigation canal, and superintended its digging. Since the water did not distribute itself, he took over the hard and thankless task of saying which field should have water at which time, piously and justly administering in the name of the highest god of the most ancient village. But power is power in whatever name, and surely only a niggard would begrudge such a savior of the state and good public servant a little reward of his hard labor! Nay more, all just and pious ones must even insist that he who represented them before the god himself must be well fed and richly dressed, and even go attended with lesser priests and with harp-players! (And, as when I wrote of the first battles of the hunters, so I can only say again, Ho-hum! and also—alas!)

Thus something new arose, and I, Man, no longer attained my greatest complexity of life in the village. I may call this whole new unit, vaguely, a district. In area it might be small, perhaps not more than ten miles square, consisting mostly of farming land, with some pasturage and bits of unreclaimed swamp. On the fertile plain stood a number of villages—ten, twenty, perhaps fifty, if the district was a large one.

If you went to look at one of these villages, you would think them much the same as the earlier ones, or somewhat better—the houses more firmly built, the animals more numerous, the tools more cleanly fashioned. There were plows, and even carts. You saw people wearing copper rings and bracelets, and using a few copper knives.

If you looked at the people working, there would be, for all you could see, no great obvious differences from earlier villages. The fathers were doing the farming; the mothers, most of their old tasks. There was still a headman and a village priest, and within the village one father of a family was still about as good as another. In some ways the headman and priest were more important than before—especially the priest, for the villagers had begun to think less for themselves and to be more superstitious about having all the proper rites performed. You might see statues indicating that their religion had taken on a grossness in which the fertility of fields and animals and people was all mixed up together.

In other ways, the headman and priest were less important than before, because the village itself was less independent, and few decisions had to be made. The ways of cultivating the fields had long since been worked out, and from year to year only small details could be referred to headman or priest. And all the outside contacts were no longer in the hands of the villagers.

Thus, for all that you could see as you looked around, there was little difference. But in the minds and hearts of the villagers, there was great change. So perhaps you might notice, if you spoke to one of them, that he dropped his eyes, and looked ill at ease, and shuffled in his speech. For he no longer was altogether a freeman, but was becoming a peasant, and already it might be said, "He is only a villager."

But who will speak so condescendingly? Surely not the hunter or the starveling nomad? No, those will be the words of the townsman.

The town, that new thing—the town has put the village down from its high estate. Already perhaps you may call it a city, so rapid has been its growth from the beginnings. The city with its surrounding villages and their lands now forms the district; or, if you prefer, you may call it a nation, though a small one. Unlike the simple village, it will exist for a long time, growing bigger and more various, pyramiding into city-state, and kingdom, and empire—but not changing basically.

First of all, as you approach the city, you see it surrounded by a wall, for defense obviously against people, not against wild animals. This, then, you must always remember—just as the village seems to have been founded on peace, so was the city founded on war! Entering through the gate, you must enter only in spirit, for already a guardsman stands there to see that no suspicious-looking foreigners pass the wall. Inside, most of the houses look much like village houses, but that must never confuse you for a moment, for a city is not at all an overgrown village.

Of the people you see in the narrow streets, only a few are farmers, those whose fields happen to lie just outside the walls. You may see some of these in the streets, and also other farmers who have come in to barter some products. But most of the people are of other kinds. There are potters, makers of stone tools, coppersmiths, carpenters. There are fishermen and fishmongers, ass-drivers, traders, and dealers in all sorts of wares. You may see a sailor who can tell you of foreign parts and strange peoples, for hasn't he voyaged a hundred miles up-river and nearly as far down? You meet priests also—and no mere villagers who dabble a little with magic in their spare time; these priests are professionals, sophisticated gentlemen, wearing amulets and special rich robes of their own to mark them. There are big fellows too, walking solidly, daggers of copper flashing from their belts; you put them down for guardsmen off duty. You may see a foreigner, black-skinned or fair-haired. There are others too, strange new sorts—courtesans (I use a polite word), beggars, and shifty fellows who look as if they never did a day's work but dealt in robbery or fleecing or throat-cutting.

Yes, a strange place, and not without interest. A bullock-sledge passes, crowding everyone to the side; it bears grain in sacks. You might even see a captain of the guard drive by in that strange new contraption—a wheeled chariot pulled by harnessed asses.

Even stranger than the vehicles are the customs. There passes one fellow walking at his ease twiddling his thumbs, and right behind (certainly following him) comes another who is bowed beneath a burden, his leg muscles standing out taut at every step. But his companion walks ahead, and offers him no help. And there is a big fellow being cruelly beaten with a stick by a little fellow. What magic of the Other-world is this? Why does not the big one turn on the little one, and beat *him*?

As you walk, you wonder perhaps what keeps all this strangeness together. Already you are sure that so many and so different people cannot work together in the simple ways of hunters and villagers. Then, getting nearer the center you see, if this is a usual city, two great buildings rising high above all the others. There is the answer as to what holds it all together.

The buildings are the palace and the temple, although it might be perhaps a palace-temple. There is the seat of power, or the two seats. Arrangements differ between cities. Commonly enough a king shares power with a high-priest, and already there is the alliance and division between the secular and the religious arms, which is not yet dead in my world. In some places the two may come together as a king-priest, or even (it may be thought) a king-god. The priest may be higher than the king, or the power may be vested in a council of priests. Or, instead of the king, there may be a group of nobles or great men.

But whether the ruler is one or two or fifty, it is all the same. Restrained only by custom, the word of the ruler is law. No longer can any two men outweigh any one, but now one outweighs a hundred or ten thousand, and commands them, and lives by the straining of their muscles.

Thus they of the cities soon came to use a new trick of power, and of another kind—not power over animals or things—but power over men!

20

It begins to slow down

YOU MAY take this present chapter as centering somewhere around 4000 B. C. This was the period of the declining village and the rising city, the two being one and the same thing. I can only say that the chapter is "centering" at a certain time, because the same kind of events were happening over a long period of years and at different times in different places.

Once before, I summoned up an imaginary philosopher and student of humanity, and decided that back before the revolution of food-production he would have made a very incorrect prophecy. At 4000 B. C., also, I think he could have used good reasoning, based on good knowledge, and again have been wrong. Recalling all the change of the last several thousand years, he would suppose that still more and faster change lay in the near future. "I feel confident about it," he might say, "because the individuals now have more security and leisure, and the best minds are gathering together into cities where they will stimulate one another."

Things failed to work out in that way, however. The

great period of change and innovation was that of the villages; as the cities developed, the rate of change began to fall off. There were indeed some important and rather showy achievements. As commerce developed, the merchants needed larger animals than asses, and they probably saw to the first taming and training of camels. (Though the camel became of greatest importance as the chief animal of the desert-nomads, such tribes cannot exist without the camel and therefore could not have first tamed it. The domesticated camel produced the Bedouin, and not the other way round.)

The people along the Indus tamed the elephant. This greatest of animals would have been merely an expense and a nuisance to villagers; I can scarcely imagine any use they would have had for elephants. But the rulers of cities used them for pomp and ceremony, for war, and for labor on public works.

This period also probably saw the taming of the horse. Horses, however, had originally nothing to do with the cities. They seem to have been used far off on the northern grasslands, first probably as meat-animals and for the mares' milk. Next they were trained to pull war-chariots, and for riding.

There was much advance also in knowledge of metals. Bronze no longer came merely by accident, when some impurities happened to get into the copper. Instead, the metal-workers learned to mix tin with copper in the right proportion. This has even been called the Age of Bronze, but like the other older terms, this one also puts too much emphasis upon one thing. At this time stone was still the common material for the farmer's tools; copper remained in use; bronze was a luxury for weapons and ornaments.

In this period merchants and priests, who were often merchant-priests, also developed the art of writing. This, however, was of such peculiar importance that I must give it a special chapter in the proper place.

Along with writing, and again the work of priests and merchants, came numerals. Since written numerals make calculation much easier, mathematics also developed, and the working out of calendars and some study of astronomy. In Egypt the priests studied astronomy to be able to predict from the position of the stars about when the rise of the Nile could be expected. There is reason to believe, because a certain cycle of the stars is involved, that they began these calculations in the year 4236 B. C. If so, that is the first event in my story which can as yet be assigned to a particular year.

All these new discoveries taken together are far from negligible, and the period was certainly not decadent. Nevertheless, when I compare these achievements with those of the village-period, I am not so much impressed. They lacked originality, and were really just the working-out of what had already been started. Domestication of the camel could follow the model of the domestication of the ass. The individuals who first got the idea and discovered the secret of working copper were much more creative than the later ones who merely perfected a method for making bronze.

In social change this era of city-growth was more active. For this reason I might hail this as one of the great creative periods, if it were not that in more recent years its two great social innovations have been somewhat discredited. They were—first, slavery; second, conquest.

I use slavery as the most convenient and general word to describe the whole system which sprang up, once the old democracy of the villagers began to fail. Slavery was to be the basis of civilization for 5000 years; in some ways it has continued strong; looking the whole world over, some people would say that it dominates even yet.

Perhaps I should have called this chapter *Further Domestication.* Just as the wild ass and the wild camel were choked into submission, so also it went with men. They were not domesticated to be companions and watchers like the dog, or to be a food-supply like the pig—but like the ass, to furnish power.

Sometimes, as when long caravans of porters toiled across desert and mountain, the slave was the mere bearer of a burden. Or, marshaled into a great gang and urged on by a whip, he pulled at ropes to drag stones up the ramp of a pyramid. But the slave had the great advantage of being able to exert his power in more skilled and delicate ways. An ass could not be trained, even after many lashings, to dig in the narrow mine-shafts for copper-ore, but a slave could. Slaves dug ditches and harvested crops and built temples. They did tasks involving much brain-power—as artisans, clerks, and stewards. They were the overseers of other slaves. But even if one rose to be a vizier, he might remain a slave only. And that meant that he was not, like a freeman, an end in himself, but was considered to exist, like the ass, only for the good of his master.

Thus in the complex life of all the ancient cities, slavery

remained essential and unchallenged. Philosophers and prophets now and then tried to soften its horrors, but they did not question the thing itself—for all their own minds were encompassed within it, and they could not imagine a world without it. So they accepted it—Plato and St. Paul alike.

According to some ways of thought, in certain places and in certain periods at least, everyone was actually a slave to the god-king. But in practice things did not work out in such a way, and a small upper-class usually kept some freedom of choice. At the same time there remained a slight distinction between the peasant who was bound to the soil, and the actual slave. The peasant was descended from the old villagers, and lived on the land of his ancestors. He might feel himself a little superior to the slave, although he was really worse off than the valued slaves who worked as household servants and held posts of trust.

If I were writing as a social reformer, I might of course grow very indignant over this reduction of the freeman to the status of a belabored domestic animal. But being what I am, I get somewhat confused about it all. Perhaps nothing else could have happened under the circumstances, so that no one is particularly to be blamed. One thing which may have had much to do with the change was the increase of population. In no country was there room for limitless expansion, and a particular field could not be made indefinitely to produce more and more food. So eventually there may have come a time when the number of mouths began to exceed the food to fill them. At such a point, there could be only two outcomes, while the state of knowledge remained what it was at that time. First, all the people could share and share alike. The result would be that they got along fairly well in good years, and then died by thousands in time of poor crops. Everyone, by such an arrangement, would live at the bare level of existence, and all the power which the villagers had got over the outside world would be of little use in helping them to live better. They would all live like slaves, and they would really be slaves—not to any human master, but to earth and sun and rain. I cannot see that this would have been a happy solution.

The other solution—and this was how it actually worked out—was that most of the people became slaves, or peasants at best; they lived poorly even in good years, and starved wholesale in famines. But a few people lived well all the time, and developed what is called civilization.

The practical choice may thus have been whether *most* people became slaves, or *all* people became slaves. What actually happened may have been the less of the two evils.

For whatever reason, slavery certainly sprang up in all the regions where cities developed. Captives in fights against marauding border-tribes may have been the first slaves, for in Mesopotamia an early word for slave meant *captive-in-war*. A supply also came from the backward peoples around the margins, often taken in organized slave-hunts. For this reason, the getting of more slaves became a chief inducement to war, and slave-trading became an industry.

The more slaves brought in from the outside, the worse competition they produced for the peasants, and the harder became the peasants' lot. Rather than have children die in famine, fathers and mothers sold them into slavery, and they might sell their ancestral lands and even themselves, just to escape immediate death from starvation. A rich merchant piled up wheat and barley in his granary, when they were cheap, and then waited for the year of famine. Even a king's minister was not above such hard practice, as the usually forgotten latter part of the story of Joseph shows too well.

Thus arose the system of classes which has been so often compared to a pyramid—at the bottom the mass of slaves, and not much above them the peasants, then sloping up through the artisans and merchants and nobles and priests to the king at the top. But really, in most of the ancient kingdoms no pyramid could represent what existed. Rather, we should think of a broad flat-topped mound representing the slaves and peasants, and in its center a spike-like pinnacle to stand for the nobles and priests, with the king again at the top. For there was generally no important middle class, and a simple pyramid cannot show the contrast between the mass of the lower people and the small number of the higher ones.

The second great social discovery of this age (if it can be called "social" and not "anti-social") was the perfection of the technique of conquest. To explain, I should first distinguish conquest from the raid, which was very old already and differed little from hunting. In hunting, you descended suddenly upon a flock of wild sheep, killed some and carried them off to eat. In a simple raid, you descended suddenly upon a village, killed some of their tame sheep, and perhaps the shepherd for good measure, and again carried the sheep off to eat. The raid grew in complexity and size as villages grew larger and more numerous. The more civilized might raid the less civilized, especially to capture slaves; more commonly, the less civilized tribes raided the more civilized. After the nomads got the use of the camel and horse they moved faster, and so they became more accomplished raiders.

But the object of the raid was not to hold permanently, only to seize control long enough to collect plunder and then to get away as quickly as possible. The raiders, to be sure, developed a technique. They were often wantonly destructive and frightful, and laid waste where they could not carry off. In doing so, they acted partly from what might be called "animal spirits," and partly from practical ends. The disorganization caused by the burning of a village cut down the chance of quick pursuit. Besides, if the people of the plundered village were massacred, the warriors from the other villages would be likely to pause in their pursuit when they saw the bodies artistically disembowelled, and they might find themselves growing cold, and return home.

But conquest was something essentially different from the raid. It must also be distinguished from the very ancient process of occupation, in which you merely drove out or killed off the original inhabitants and lived in the region yourself. Conquest, however, involved subjecting the people as well as their country. In its full technique it came to show three parts: to take, to hold, and to make profitable.

Who first made the discovery cannot be known—or when, or where. Yet most likely it was not extremely old. It was probably younger than the idea of slavery, for conquest was really a kind of mass-enslavement, involving a change of masters.

Probably the full technique could not develop until after the city-kingdom had come into being, along with slavery. Then, to take, the one king and his army only had to crush the other kind and *his* army, and this could often be done in a single battle. To hold, the victorious king made sure that the other king and his chief nobles were dead; he himself was then king of two cities instead of one, and could set up some of his own nobles in the conquered city. To make profitable, the new king and his nobles collected and used the income of their second city.

The slaves and peasants and domestic animals passed from one master to another without trouble and without necessarily any change for better or worse. The peasants often realized this, and so they sometimes continued with their plowing or harvesting while the battle raged in full sight.

Some kings of course did not understand the true nature of conquest, but they were really backward ones who kept to the old psychology of the raid. So they plundered and burned and killed, and disrupted the life of the villages so badly that they could not make the conquest profitable. Often conquest tended to get mixed up with the three R's of religion, race-prejudice, and revenge; when it did, it became less skillful conquest.

To observe the work of a real master, we can look

at the career of Alexander the Great, who went into the business later, at a time when its methods were well developed. To take, he had first to defeat the Persian army. To hold, he had to kill the Persian king, and so he went to great pains to insure doing so. Then he made as little disturbance as possible in ways of life; he even paid his respects to local gods, and built temples to them. He destroyed as little as possible, for a devastated country is no use to anyone. After that, to make profitable was easy, for he was no longer mere king of small and barren Macedon, but he was King of Kings and able to enjoy the profits of the civilized world.

I have mentioned Alexander, even though I had to skip ahead in the story to do so. But he furnishes a good example of conquest at its best. In such conquest, there was little change of population, and the actual disturbance in way of life might amount to almost nothing—scarcely more than a change of fashion, sometimes less than occurred with a change of dynasty.

To the ruling classes, conquest had all the importance of the shift from rags to riches, or from glorious estate to miserable death. The general idea of conquest is thus of great importance in my story. By dominating the kings and nobles it in a sense dominated history. It was the true Sport of Kings, and the first Big Business. It was speculative, for anyone going in for it risked his life. But it could yield tremendous profits. Therefore, how to conquer and how to avoid being conquered became in themselves dominating ideas.

Yet the individual conquests are of very little importance in my story. The kings went forth to battle by many names—Thothmes and Rameses, Sargon and Nebuchadnezzar, Henry, and Frederick, and Louis. They fought at the river-fords, or by the slime-pits, or in the passes—at Kadesh and Armageddon, at Carchemish and Troy, at Agincourt and Blenheim. After the famous victory, one king replaced another—nothing more, except sometimes a poem or a story. It was the flurry of waves in a pond, where the level was left unchanged. In all this welter of kings and kingdoms, I can only think of the words of my Frenchman, "The more it changes, the more it remains the same thing!"

21

Of my individuals again

The jolting shift from free villages to a city-kingdom with its dependent villages greatly affected the life of my individuals, and perhaps even the individuals themselves. And here for the first time I must make a distinction of classes. Previously I had to talk only of such natural divisions as fathers, mothers, and children. But now it becomes strange—almost as if I, Man, lost my identity, and split into two parts, as happens sometimes with the diseased mind of an individual. And just as that individual begins to suffer strains and peculiar torments, so also (in a manner of speaking) it happened with me also.

After the masters on the one hand had drawn apart from the slaves and peasants on the other, a natural development would have been for things to go even further, each group marrying only within itself, until the two gradually diverged and came to differ as much as beef-cattle from milch-cattle. Some romancers have even imagined a world in which this occurred. But actually it never took place. One reason why it did not, I think, was that kings and nobles were always ready to take beautiful concubines from the lower classes; occasionally also, as in the story of Potiphar's wife, a great lady might fall in love with a slave—and certainly not all male slaves were of Joseph's mind in such matters. Again, as the story of Joseph also illustrates, a talented or lucky slave might now and then rise to power, and win a high-born wife.

Also, no one seems to have worked out the idea (although someone certainly must have had it) that slaves could be bred for special purposes, as domestic animals were. But though the horse was bred for speed and the sheep could hardly have developed his long unnatural fleece without help, still no one bred a race of slaves with stupid docile minds and strong bodies. Probably all that prevented it was that their long childhood made the process too slow, so that the individual slave-owner could never have carried the experiment through more than two or three generations in his own lifetime. The separation thus remained one of the ways of life and thought, and was not fully confirmed in the blood.

As an individual, the slave or peasant came to correspond to his way of life. He worked long and hard at monotonous labor, and sometimes:

Stolid and stunned, a brother to the ox,

he became more brutalized than the savage or barbarian. He won no advantage by being more enterprising, or by doing things efficiently, or by having new ideas; any increased production went, immediately or in the long run, to the master. There was no reason why he should work to stand out from the crowd; quite the contrary, for the outstanding slave or peasant, especially if he seemed to be a leader, merely put himself in danger of a flogging, or worse.

If a people are forced to live in a forest, they either die off, or else in the course of generations become adjusted and live in the thick woods with much contentment; they even gaze out with fear and disgust, and tell frightening stories about the wide grasslands where the sun shines and anyone must walk with that dangerous thing, a shadow, dogging him. Such a group of beliefs, passed down from parents to children, growing stronger, often becomes tied up with religion. At least it becomes a whole system of thought, or what is called an *ideology*. And an ideology, continuing through centuries, may shape the life of a people or a class of people almost as much as if their actual minds and bodies had changed.

So it went with those of the lower classes in the ancient cities and the villages surrounding them. Work kept the body busy, but demanded little of the brain. Such work, the fulfillment of the daily duty, came even to bring satisfaction. Their minds began to fear independent action and, like their bodies, to love the protecting shelter of the crowd. Merely to be one of many was safest, and what is safest is always close to being what is best. Thus for the first time a whole body of people came to approach, in their ways of thought, not the wolf-pack, but the flock of sheep. That peasant lived most contentedly (I can hardly say "happily") who was most like all the others.

Naturally, therefore, the peasants disliked all innovation, and became tradition-ridden. Living so much as one of a group, they did not understand, and so hated and feared, anyone from outside. Their religion built up the basic justification: "As we do, that is right!" And so the peasant, being only comfortable with the familiar, sometimes even fought desperately in defense of the system which oppressed him.

Servility also, something new in my life, now developed —the doffing of the cap; the standing with lowered eyes; the saying "Your lordship . . ." And, in compensation, then developed also the arts of low cunning, of petty deception, of saying, "Yes, master, count it already as good as done!" with the satisfaction that once his back is turned it need not be done.

The greatest final result of all this was to make the individual sink back into the crowd. More than in a hunters' band or a free village, the peasants acted alike, and so for practical purposes *were* alike. In personality the village tended to become poverty-stricken.

And what of the upper classes? May I see in them everything opposite—initiative, love of new things, richly varied personality? Not as much, I fear, as anyone at first might think. Every lord, though he might seem all-powerful to his slave, felt himself little better than a slave in the presence of the king. There is an old tale of the king who went to a wise man for advice. The wise man said nothing, but as he walked in the field he struck off with his staff every head of grain which stood higher than the others. For this reason the lords also found comfort in remaining one of the crowd.

They had of course more chance than slaves or peasants to develop personality, just as the captain of a hundred generally used more initiative than one of his spearmen. A priest might dabble in science or philosophy. He might even develop a little skepticism of the gods, provided he did not let it interfere with his proper bowing in the temple. He might be the patron of artists, and would even compose a poem himself, although anything as mechanically laborious as the painting of a picture he left to his slaves.

As with the priest, so also it might be with any gentleman—civil servant, plantation-owner, or warrior. In more serious and outward matters he conformed, and lived by the traditions of the fathers.

At the very top was the king, whatever name he might be called. He had fullest power to develop his personality as he wished. Yet when everyone else was tied by tradition, he himself was also much bound by custom of conformity; he would usually have no desire to act in any other way than his fathers had done. So he too usually expressed his personality within the conventional limits—on the battlefield, at the feasting-table, and in the harem. In fact he can seldom have had the imagination to realize that much in his life could be more to his liking, and so he had little desire for change.

Thus, it happened, the shift from the village to the city brought no enrichment of personality, but rather the contrary. From the bottom, looking upwards, individuals were slaves and peasants and subjects; they approved of likeness and gave up individuality for the servile safety of the crowd. Looking downwards, individuals were masters and despots.

Wherever peasants and slaves still exist in the world (and there are many millions), they will understand and feel at one with those first peasants and slaves. Wherever masters and despots exist (and there are still many of them), they will be at one with those first masters and despots. But where freemen live together, they will feel no kinship with either slave or despot, and will feel the life of those cities strange to them. To find kinship they must look farther back—to the days of village freemen.

22

"—it remains the same thing!"

But whether anyone likes or dislikes that civilization of cities, he must admit that it was a highly practical way of life. By that very resistance to change, it preserved itself unchanged. It remained the only known form of civilization throughout most of the period of history. Even yet it still exists basically unchanged in many places. Nowhere in the world probably have people as yet got wholly out of their minds the first idea of this civilization —that some should be lords (or ends in themselves) and others should be slaves (or means to the end).

The resistance of this civilization to change is thus basic in my whole story. I have explained something about it in the last chapter, and I shall make its why-and-wherefore the subject of this one.

Why the slaves and peasants could make no changes is obvious enough. Why the kings and priests and nobles were so uncreative is harder to explain, but as I have suggested, it may rest upon what I call "the finite individual." By this I mean that an individual cannot have an unlimited number of desires and that these desires cannot be bottomless. He can, for instance, eat only a certain amount of food. After the cities were well established, an upper-class person had all he could possibly eat and drink. He found himself surrounded by comfort and luxury. Slaves waited upon him. He satisfied his senses in all ways. Everything he wanted, he had. What was still undiscovered, he did not know about and so could not actually want. Why should he desire to change things? He would have been a fool if he had!

Between the upper and the lower, there was only a weak and unimportant middle class of master-artisans and merchants. They alone had some desire and some opportunity for change. And if everything were known, probably most of the few changes which occurred during this time sprang from them.

But even the artisans and merchants must have been overwhelmed with tradition, setting its face against change. Tradition is one of those many two-edged tools. It is of tremendous advantage, I see that clearly enough, in that through it an individual absorbs in his short lifetime so much of the experience which the race has acquired from the beginning—everything from language and the use of fire down to the latest improvements in the plow.

But tradition always looks backward. It tells how things were done well enough in the past, how old problems were solved. It gives little guidance as to how things may be done better in the future, as to how new problems are to be solved. The overwhelming majority of individuals in any age also, I think, agree with tradition in being conservative. They enjoy living in the good old way. Something from the outside, such as a shift of climate, may force them to change. Or a startling invention like the bow may throw off the balance, and begin a long period of change before the balance is restored.

Thus, as I have said before, "Change breeds change." By implication, the proverb means also its opposite, "Stability breeds stability." And that means that once a way of life has remained stable for a century, it will be even more resistant to change, and so on and on.

In the cities, before so very long, this idea of stability began to develop into an ideology. As people looked back and, lacking history, saw no evidence of change, they assumed naturally that their unchanging way of life had been once created as it was, had not changed since, and was not going to change. Thus the Babylonians believed of the ancient fish-shaped god: "Oannes left to the people all things that make life better, and since that time nothing new has been invented."

Since many individuals, growing older, looked back to childhood and youth with rosy memories, they came to think that, if anything, civilization was slipping a little. Thus grew up the idea that a golden age once existed, and that if things were at all bad they should be made better by a return to the virtues of the past.

One thing with another, there is thus no reason to be greatly surprised at the lack of change. Once the cities were really well established, from about 2500 B. C., the changes affected merely the fringes of life—that is, they were connected only with those small departments where the king and the upper classes had a desire for change.

First of all, there came a striking development in the minor field of refinements and luxury. This shows itself particularly in art. I do not mean to say that art is a minor matter. But actually in this period the sum-total of creative expression was very likely sinking. Folk-art was declining, and specialists, often slaves, centered around the court. These professionals were naturally more skillful than the amateur villagers who puttered about modeling figurines and carving bones. Also these new artists had more and richer materials for working with. Many of the more durable of these new productions have come down to the present: buildings and tombs, statues and carvings, pottery and faience, fine bits of metal-work, glass, mummy-cases and other wood-work, ivories, occasional wall-paintings, and even works of literature. Much else we learn at second-hand. We do not know the tunes or the steps, but we can see musicians and dancers in a carved relief. So also we need not doubt that there were story-tellings and recitations, pageants and rituals which passed into drama, professional games and exhibitions, contests of skill, fine cookery. Along with all this came increase in knowledge and advance in skill.

Whether there was really any advance in artistic feeling is another matter. And in any case, all this art was for the few. If the peasants ever saw any of it, they probably just gaped in wonder without really appreciating its sophistication.

No one country could produce all the rare and much-desired materials. So trade developed. Caravans and ships went out to other cities or to less civilized tribes who might have gold or furs to barter, or rare spices or magical herbs. Thus after 2500 B. C. sailing-vessels and the art of navigation still continued developing. The whole Cretan state grew up by its people learning to follow the ways of the sea. On land, there was not much change; the porter, the ass, and the camel formed the caravans. On the whole, these traders seem to have developed little that was new, but they at least spread around what was already known. They also enlarged geographical knowledge in a practical way.

Something more that the kings wanted was a knowledge of the future. Their desires here led generally to nothing important—a lot of hocus-pocus about gazing at the entrails of sacrificed animals, and consulting oracles. In Mesopotamia, however, the priests had probably learned at a very early time to predict the change of the seasons by the position of the stars. Since the stars thus tied up with such important matters as the coming of the rains and the time for planting crops, any reasonable person might assume that they were tied up with other important matters also. Trying to discover the connection and put it to use as astrology, the priests studied the stars and learned more about astronomy and the calendar.

Most of the changes of the city-period, however, were tied up with war. No matter how often his courtiers told the king, and his poets sang, that he was invincible, still he might come up against disillusion on the battlefield. So even the most conservative king and upper class could not remain too conservative in weapons and tactics, or they were overthrown. For this reason, the chief change which was likely to come in with a conqueror was a change connected with war. As has happened in later times, war thus pioneered with many new inventions, and was probably the most active force working against utter conservatism. Bronze and iron were first used for weapons; the horse and the elephant were war-engines; the wheel had an important development in connection with the chariot. (But even in matters of war, the kings and nobles were sometimes foolishly conservative. Marathon showed the Persians, and Plataea rubbed the lesson in, that Greek spearmen could defeat many times their number of equally brave Persian bowmen and cavalry. Yet the Persians never learned to fight in the Greek manner, and after a century of refusing to learn they lost their empire, chiefly for that very reason.)

In spite of all this settling into the dullness of stability, the period had a certain brilliance because of the flowering of professional art. By the biological test also, it can be called successful, for the number of individuals must still have been increasing. By harder and harder work the peasants got bigger yields from the fields. Around the edges they reclaimed more fields from the desert-margin. With every increase in the villages, the cities also grew larger.

Thus they arose in a size and complexity and brilliancy which, a short time before, no one could even have beheld in a dream—Thebes, the hundred-gated; Ur of the Chaldees; Babylon, the glory of kingdoms; Nineveh; labyrinthine Cnossos; the Great City Shang; Mohenjo-Daro; Sushan-the-palace. Even yet the thought of them stirs the blood, and their names are poetry.

23

I come into the light of history

WITH the discovery of writing, my story "comes into the light of history," and there must be a certain change in my methods of telling it. I hope that the change will not be too great, and especially that I shall not let the later part of my story become long-winded merely because the invention of writing has produced so many particular and interesting details. Historians who are trained to work from written records, put all my life *before* writing into a kind of grudging introductory chapter, and then with relief settle down really to tell the tale after they can name names and date dates. Anthropologists and archeologists, however, generally spend all their pages on my story *before* writing. They seldom consider how pre-history developed into and through history; or if they do, it is likely to be by a kind of postscript corresponding to the historians' introductory chapter. In short, I am afraid, each of them according to his specialty is a student of a certain kind of evidence, not of my whole story.

I, Man, am trying to keep my eye on the story itself, whatever the kind of evidence. Just how many pages should be apportioned to this or that period is of course a great problem. But at least I see the difficulty, and am trying to keep proportions according to what I consider the importance of the various parts. In particular, I shall try from this point to keep the story from expanding too much.

In itself, writing was not a very amazing invention. For all anyone knows, among those clever draughtsmen, the stone-age Aurignacians, the scouts may have drawn pictures and pointers on rocks as a way of passing back information to their comrades who followed—and that is a good step in the direction of writing. The real development, however, followed the growth of cities, and the merchants must have had much to do with it. Merchants certainly were people who had the need to send long-distance messages and to keep records and accounts. But in the early cities merchants were often priests, and priests in turn were often administrators of the city. So from its start, writing must have developed in connection with religion and statecraft also.

Writing, like so much else, seems to have been worked out by easy stages. First came the picture, then the simplified and conventional picture like a stick-drawing. Finally this simplified picture came to stand for the word instead of the thing. Then some kind of simplified picture or conventional symbol represented by common custom some word which in itself could not be surely drawn, such as *indebted* or *after*.

The invention of an alphabet came later, and as yet cannot be traced back beyond 1500 B. C. As an invention, it seems more remarkable than the earlier phases of writing, for it called for the ability to analyze and abstract the sounds which composed a word.

The alphabet, however, was not nearly so important as the earlier developments. Some peoples, like the Chinese, flowered brilliantly and got along for thousands of years with a kind of picture-writing. Theoretically, the alphabet made everything so easy that almost anyone could learn to read and write. Actually, through the centuries, alphabet or no alphabet, reading and writing remained the speciality of scribes or a small educated class. Slaves, peasants, and many of the upper classes also, especially the women, remained as illiterate as apes.

Writing was speech adapted to the needs of time and space. By writing messages, people could talk from a distance more at length and more accurately than by sending a message by word of mouth. Also, writing preserved the record of speech, so that the present could refer back to the past with certainty and could pass its own information on to the future.

This conquest of time was much more important than the corresponding conquest of space, for it permitted the development of co-operation between individuals. Without writing, the life in a large city might soon have lapsed into utter confusion. There could be little certainty about laws and regulations, about taxes paid or to be paid, about agreements and contracts. Writing gave the scrupulous their best protection against the unscrupulous. It was at least a check on indiscriminate tyranny, and under indiscriminate tyranny any city soon grew demoralized and went to pieces. As a general rule, the state or institution or person that most carefully kept written records was the most honest, for it was much more practical to keep vague records or none at all than to undertake the dangerous process of manufacturing false records. (Even the early Babylonians learned the value of duplicate copies, although I do not know that they went so far as triplicate or quadruplicate on different colored clay.)

Thus, though everyone rails about red tape, I find myself forced to say a good word for it. I think that no one would buy stock in a company unless it sent him a stock-certificate and unless he believed that an immediate and careful record of his purchase was made in the books. Who, ancient or modern, ever wanted to go without getting a receipt for his taxes, or at least knowing that the payment had been recorded? For this reason, business and government and even religion rarely developed much beyond village or tribal simplicity without the aid to morale which the keeping of the records supplies.

Writing was also important in other ways. It was an excellent preserver and spreader of all kinds of knowledge. Since its beginning, whenever friends were separated, the writing of letters made glad the heart of sender and receiver. Writing gave to the individual an improved means of expression. Oral poetry was good enough, but it was like the flower which faded while you watched—its continuing existence as uncertain as the flickering life of a new-born infant. Its maker himself, in a little while, might forget just how the lines had gone. If it spread to the lips of many men and lasted through the generations, it changed as it went. But Horace told only the literal truth, or even less than that, when he wrote that his poem was a monument more lasting than bronze. For, in its chance of immortality the written word is like gold or sapphire. If lost, it vanishes, and generally does not live on in some baser form. Even if it is broken to pieces, the fragments still shine with the original sparkle.

Although writing thus supplied much to make my story interesting, it also worked strongly, I am afraid, to prevent change and thus keep the story dull. Oral tradition might be hampering, although it had a tendency to shift a little as it went along through the generations. But writing tremendously reinforced all the elements which were working against change. (And what is any good story but a record of change?)

Since the authority of the written word in contract or receipt was final, so also any written word came to bear the suggestion of finality. Also, from the beginning, writing had something of hocus-pocus and magic about it—that far-distant or dead people could talk with those present! To believe something because it was in writing, particularly if the writing was ancient, became a fixed habit of most individuals.

Sometimes this exposed them to the trickery of forgers, but that was not the worst. The greatest danger was that reverence for writing put the world too much under the control of the dead hand of the past. An Egyptian of 2900 B. C. wrote a treatise on surgery, and some centuries later this was not only a text-book, but a kind of Bible.

The later Egyptians thus deferred to this godlike wisdom of the fathers, accepted its error along with its soundness, and learned nothing new. The most intelligent and intellectual people were the very ones who learned writing. They were the ones who should have led the way to new discoveries of all kinds, but they were also the ones who, by reading, fell most under the sway of the past, as writing preserved it.

In both directions, writing was the most basic craft of the city-civilization. Without it, there could scarcely have been that growth in the size of the community and all the resulting complexities of government, religion, and business. On the other hand, writing was one of the most important forces in producing conservatism, and stopping any further essential change. For, certainly, that mere growth in size and complexity was only a matter of quantity, not of quality.

Still I cannot leave the subject of writing. It had, or was to have, another effect, and perhaps the most important of all. This was not even to be apparent until after many centuries, and no one would realize its full importance until after several thousands of years. By this I mean that writing preserved the historical record of what I was doing, and thus in the end raised me to feel a new dignity and to have a new respect for myself. Before writing, I was a kind of homeless and timeless waif, a chip afloat on the flowing river of the years, senseless of what had passed, unconscious that anything different might come. In an uncovered grave a villager might see a skull and thigh-bones, old-fashioned pots, and stone knives. But he could not know whether they were a hundred or a hundred thousand years old. He did not know that their crude and out-of-date forms represented the best that his ancestors could do at the time. If I may put it so without too much confusion of pronouns, let me say: "He did not know my true greatness."

This is well seen in the creation-myths, which were developing by the time of the early cities. These placed my creation back some distance, usually not very far. In them, I was imagined a kind of favored child of some god, born with a gold spoon in my mouth, not like the animals. Then the work of establishing civilization in its various details was credited to a god or demi-god, like Marduk or Prometheus. This did me great injustice, and it is something about which I feel bitter. For I was no well-born child, but am self-made. I, Man, not the demigod Prometheus, got the use of fire. No Marduk, but I, Man—*my own brain and hands*—produced civilization!

All this may seem a long way from writing, but it is not. Until individuals through writing had got a feeling for Man in time, for the long course of history, they had little chance to approach the vastly more difficult study of pre-history, which is so much longer, and in which I made the most and greatest of my achievements.

History in the narrower sense springs directly from the written record, and cannot really exist without it. The record of archeology is equally important, and interesting, but it differs in kind. For in history we have the drama of the particular, and the emergence of the event and the individual. Thus we may learn from the daily record kept by his scribes that Thothmes, king of Egypt, marched out from Zalu toward Palestine on April 19th, in the year 1479 B. C.; and a very interesting story can be made of that campaign too. Read all about it! Great victory at Megiddo!

So also the other individuals appear. There is Father Abraham (I care not if he is partly fictional) with his longing for a son, and his troubles and his weaknesses, and the essential well-meaning and decency of him showing through in everything he did. And there is Isaac his son, more hazily seen and romantically. You can read his love-story still, with its curious tenderness for the watering of the camels, as if the camel-driver himself were telling it. Or, in Babylon, there is Hammurabi the good lawgiver, who may by twisted legend be that same Amraphel whom Abraham smote and pursued "unto Hobah, which is on the left hand of Damascus."

"Many brave men lived before Agamemnon," so also we may be sure that long before Abraham there were others just as noble. But even if we dig up their tombs, we can at best only guess it vaguely, by the shape of the skull, or the implements in the grave. Yes, there were many—gullible as old Isaac, wise and subtle as Imhotep (whom the Greeks made into Aesculapius), beautiful as Rachel, or Nefretete, or Helen, clever and shifty as Jacob.

We shall never know them, but perhaps it is just as well. There are of record a great many more individuals than anyone can keep track of. Historians have become so infatuated with them that in reading history, as I have said already, "You cannot see Man because of men." For in itself the rise of a king or the fall of a city need not be of the slightest importance. At most it is often nothing more than a rousing tale, and as such, I assert, more significant as the subject of epic and folk-tale than as part of my story. So, as I continue, I shall still keep to my purpose of telling mostly of the essential "What happened?" not of the incidental "Who did it?"

24

Inside—outside

Now that I have come into that light of history, although it is still dim and flickering, I might well look around again to see what the world was like, about 2000 B. C. There is another reason for taking such a look: what we see will not change essentially for more than three thousand years, throughout most of the course of history.

First of all, the world of about 2000 B. C. was no longer at all simple. Its varieties of ways of life and its complications were almost as extreme as they have been at any time since, ranging all the way from savagery to highly developed civilization.

At its center, like a core, lay the cities, already differing much from one another and grouped into shifting kingdoms and empires. By then the old cities of the Indus valley seem to have gone under; already they were ruins for the lion and the lizard to keep, for simple tribesmen to look at and call work of the giants. Perhaps, in compensation, cities had already sprung up elsewhere in India, and also in China; if so, they were not yet very important, and had no strong influence on my story for some time.

The centers of civilization were in Egypt and Mesopotamia. Between them a thin line of less notable cities followed the curve of well-watered country around through Palestine, Phoenicia, Syria, and Assyria. Beyond, there were outpost-cities—eastward, along the southern slope of the Iranian mountains; westward, on Crete; here and there perhaps, on other Mediterranean islands and in Asia Minor. Although all these cities shared much the same civilization, no one should think of them as presenting a united front to the outsiders. On the contrary, they were constantly waging wars of conquest, one against the other.

Even more, for a defense against the barbarians outside, the cities were at a geographical disadvantage. If any commander-in-chief had been entrusted with their defense, he would have seen that he was in a very bad strategic position—his lines strung out thinly from east to west along frontiers which wandered to the north and then back to the south again. The two chief clusters of cities were almost at the ends of the line. Even if they had wanted to, the armies of Egypt and Mesopotamia could never have come readily to each other's aid, and as for the long shoestring stretching between them, it lay wide-open to attack from north or from south.

Moreover, by this time, there were plenty of attackers, and they were of that type of people who can most conveniently be called barbarians. In general, the barbarians were tribes who had advanced some distance toward city-life without going the whole way. Moreover, they had not learned about civilization in the slow hard manner, by developing it for themselves. They had picked it up quickly by copying what Egypt and Mesopotamia had discovered for them. They learned comfortably, in peace, when they bartered their own raw products for the manufactured goods of the traders. They learned uncomfortably, in war, when the kings of the cities led armies into the back-country. Either way, their education often was rapid. Certain tribesmen in 3000 B. C. might have been living by simple hunting-and-foraging, but by 2000 B. C. they would be raising crops, keeping herds, working metals, and even owning slaves. Thus in a thousand years, or even much less, they took over as much at second-hand as it had taken several thousand years to discover.

Sometimes I can actually show how this happened. North of the Black Sea, for instance, once lived some tribesmen who came to use an improved kind of battle-ax as their favorite weapon. The trick of it was that they made a hole in the head, and thrust the handle through. This was much better than the old way, of tying the head to the handle, and for that reason it has become the regular modern way of making an ax. But the chief point is that the tribesmen did not apparently make this discovery. That was done in the Sumerian cities, a good thousand miles to the south across many mountain ranges. Through traders the tribesmen probably got some copper axes of this type, and later copied the design in stone, since they had no copper in their country. Having thus got a better weapon these "Battle-ax people" later became great conquerors.

The rule everywhere was that material things were more readily borrowed and imitated than immaterial things. The barbarians were quick enough to see the advantage of a new ax, but were less anxious to take over new ways of living. Yet the one necessarily tended to bring in the other. Metal-working meant that there had to be smiths as a special group of workers, and so there came a beginning of a class-system. To learn about domestic animals was to learn about slaves. After a while the tribal war-chiefs began to be something like kings.

Eventually this process might go on internally until a full city-civilization developed. Perhaps something of the sort happened in Crete, and in China. With most tribes, however, the ordinary tribesmen did not sink into being peasants. As a people, they had developed very rapidly from being hunters. They still kept most of the hunters' ways of thought, and passed over easily into being herdsmen and warriors. So the typical barbarian tribe raised a few crops and carried on crafts like pottery and metalwork, but relied for food largely upon flocks and herds, and considered that one of the most ordinary and profitable and honorable parts of life was—war!

At first their wars consisted of mere raids for plunder and glory. Before long, they learned the technique of conquest. Thus the Battle-ax People, for instance, spread around over a larger and larger territory.

There is no mystery about how it went. To begin with, some particular tribe lived more or less quietly on its own lands. They received the visits of traders with city-goods, and also at the convenient time of year, probably in late summer, they went out raiding against near-by tribes. Their neighbors also raided them. Eventually one tribe became restless. Perhaps its people grew too numerous for its territory, or perhaps there was a famine, or a dispute between factions, or perhaps there was too hard pressure from one direction by some other people. Then the tribe, or some part of it, poured out for conquest. Sometimes they were merely an army of adventurers; sometimes they took women and children along with them. If defeated, they became a landless and broken people, soon to vanish entirely. If victorious, they took over the new country. In that case, the victors sometimes killed or drove out the old inhabitants, but more often made them (some of them at least) into slaves and peasants, and ruled over them.

The end-point was thus not so different from the situation in the cities, for there was an arrangement into classes with usually a king at the top. But the difference, like most of those between the cities and the tribes, was one of degree. The king was more likely to be merely the first among equals, as with a hunting-tribe. The descendants of the original conquerors remained numerous and very independent in spirit; in fact, they were essentially freemen.

I have gone into the development of the barbarians somewhat in detail because in the next three thousand years, from 2000 B. C. to 1000 A. D., and even later, most of what I find worth the telling is concerned with tribes who were just ceasing to be barbarians. In the cities the pattern had become so strong that people were no longer making changes. In fact, it was so strong that, as soon as any barbarians were completely absorbed into city-life, they too ceased to be creative.

I notice something else interesting. Sometimes the city people went out, conquered barbarian lands, and brought them definitely within the circle of civilization. Thus Carthage conquered parts of barbarian Spain, and Rome conquered barbarian Gaul. When it happened thus, I fail to note any sudden flare-up of creative activity. The barbarians were probably too quickly suppressed, and since the conquerors were more highly civilized also, they imposed their own fully developed and static ways of life. Even if the conquered barbarians were more advanced in some ways, their special achievements were likely to be lost. Thus certain of the Gauls were much better seamen and navigators than the Romans, but the Romans killed most of those tribes, turned the rest of them into slaves and provincials—and perhaps put the discovery of America off for a thousand years.

But sometimes the barbarians conquered cities, and then the situation was different. The conquerors obviously had much to learn from the conquered, and yet the conquerors would not willingly or quickly give up their own ways. So there was a period, which stretched out over some centuries with certain peoples, when there was conflict of ideas, and the still-free sons and grandsons of the invaders did not know all the answers. Thus they had to keep open minds, and in the process of adjusting themselves to the older civilization they sometimes made new discoveries of their own.

To return more definitely to 2000 B. C., you will remember that the territory of the cities stretched along an east-west line. It was therefore subject to attack from north and south, and in each direction there already were warlike and talented barbarian peoples.

To the south, along the desert margins and far into Arabia, ranged the barbarian Semites. I must say "barbarian Semites" because from very early times some of the Semites had lived in Mesopotamia, and they may have been among the original developers of civilization. But there were still plenty of wild Semites left. Because they lived in dry grassland, shading into true desert, they were shepherds and nomads. In later years they held Ishmael to be their ancestor—that son of Abraham who grew up to be a wild man and an archer, "his hand against every man, and every man's hand against him." In 2000 B. C. these nomads were probably following their flocks on foot with perhaps some asses to carry their tents and water-skins. Already they were raiding the city people, but they were not very powerful. Some centuries later, when they had learned to use camels, they became much more dangerous.

Toward the north, as if counterbalancing the Semites, another great group of barbarians also began to press in. They were probably much more numerous and were certainly much more widespread and dangerous. They launched their attacks against the cities from north, northeast, and northwest, and even, somewhat later, from across the Mediterranean in ships. They also spread around during the same centuries by conquering other barbarian peoples, eastward as far as India, and far to the west and north in the region which was later to be known as Europe. This group of peoples has been called by many names, but are most often known as Indo-Europeans.

Strictly speaking, they were the speakers of a group of related languages, rather than kinsmen by blood. Yet the assumption would be that they shared some common blood. They also shared certain ways of life. For instance, they worshipped their own gods, such as the sky-god still remembered under his names Zeus and Jupiter.

Before 2000 B. C. they were not apparently a very creative people, and indeed they did not make any great contribution to the world for a long time after that date either. Possibly, before 2000 B. C., one of their tribes was the first to domesticate the horse; and possibly, somewhat after that date, another of their tribes discovered a practical way to smelt iron. But even if these two discoveries can be credited to these people, both were secondary, not primary discoveries like the domestication of the ass and the smelting of copper.

Much has been written about the mystery of the origin of the Indo-Europeans, but of course there is no mystery about it, except that nothing is known certainly—which constitutes ignorance, not mystery. Like all other peoples, they must have been descended from ancestors who were living somewhere ever since there were ground-apes. In the long run, as much is known about their ancestry as is known about that of other peoples—in short, just about what you will find in the earlier chapters of this book.

The Battle-ax People were the early Indo-Europeans or some branch of them. Just about 2000 B. C. (and that is another reason why this is an important date) various tribes began to sweep down upon the cities. The Hittites made a great raid into Mesopotamia from the northwest. The Kassites came against Babylon from the northeast, out of the Iranian mountains, and established a dynasty; they were the first known users of the horse in warfare. The Hyksos kings conquered Egypt and set up a dynasty there. The Mitanni founded a kingdom along the upper Euphrates. The Aryans, not much later, pushed down through the mountains into India.

The Aryans were an Indo-European tribe on the move, who worked ahead step by step with their wives and families, establishing themselves as they went. The Hittites were probably a warrior-aristocracy; they may or may not have brought their women along with them, and after establishing their kingdom they certainly ruled over a subject people. The Mitanni were even more of a warrior group ruling a large body of natives. As for the Kassites and Hyksos, nothing is definitely known to be Indo-European about them except the names of gods and kings; at most, their leaders were Indo-European in descent, but leading native armies, perhaps no longer even speaking their old speech, but still keeping their traditions of conquest and leadership.

Thus from their first appearance the Indo-Europeans established themselves in the double role which they were to play for several thousand years. First, they were masters of warfare, raiding, and plunder; among them a king might rejoice in the epithet: "waster of cities." But second, some of them were also masters of the full technique of conquest; they knew how to rule strongly. Even from the beginning of history, moreover, their scattered tribes recognized no kinship, and were just as ready to plunder and conquer one another as anyone else.

I have written fully of these Indo-Europeans, because the future was definitely with them. Kassites and Hyksos were driven out after a while, and along with Mitanni and Hittites disappeared from history. But others of their tribes came on: Medes, Persians, Phrygians, Achaeans. And though they ebbed back occasionally, they always came on again. As I write this page, some form of Indo-European speech is the dominating language over nearly all of the world. This is the most remarkable expansion of which I have record.

Also I find amusement in noticing how the speakers of Indo-European languages have continued their favorite occupations of conquering and ruling a people, and then leading them on in new armies. A French officer commanding a battalion of Moroccans or Senegalese is in much the situation, as far as we can tell, of a Kassite or Hyksos king.

Yet I should not close this chapter so as to leave the impression that these newcomers were only warriors and conquerors. Besides mere "wasters of cities" I number among them Zoroaster, Gautama, Asoka, Homer, Socrates, Virgil, Marcus Aurelius, Alfred, and many others whose names still burn like scattered lights beside a long dark road. Also, after three thousand years, when the long deadlock at last was broken and new life re-entered my story, that too was to be the work of peoples who sprang from these recently barbarous tribes.

25

Some tribes from the south

SHORTLY after 2000 B. C. the Hebrews made a not-too-glorious entry into history as tribesmen, barbarian Semites, inhabiting the desert-margin along the Egyptian-controlled land of Canaan, and now and then raiding the frontiers. By 1700 they were changing from raiders into conquerors, and holding some of the land which they had at first only plundered. The later-written book of *Joshua* made this conquest appear chiefly a single campaign of a single people. Actually it continued through seven centuries, and the invaders came in waves as different tribes.

This long warfare affected the Hebrews, one may say, forever. Like most tribesmen, they were not as numerous as the city-people whom they attacked; they were not even as well armed. According to their own traditions, they did not at first know how to work metal, and their southern tribes used the sling instead of the bow. The sling indeed, as the David-and-Goliath story shows, was not a bad weapon, especially in desert country where stones were plentiful; even so, after the crippling defeat at Mount Gilboa, the tribe of Judah learned the use of the bow to meet the Philistine archers on equal terms.

With numbers and weapons often both against them, the Hebrews met many defeats. When they won, it must have been because, as gaunt and hard-bitten tribesmen, they individually showed greater courage and skill and strength than their city-softened enemies. Thus they developed a warrior-tradition as fine as anything of the Spartans or Romans. In romance or epic you will read no more chivalrous tale than that of the siege of Bethlehem when David longed for water from the well by the gate, and three of his warriors heard him:

And the three broke through the host of the Philistines, and drew water out of the well by the gate, and brought it to David. But David would not drink of it, but poured it out to the Lord. And he said, "God forbid, that I should do this thing. Shall I drink the blood of these men who have risked their lives?"

When victory was possible only if each warrior did his best, the Hebrews learned to value the individual. Their fable of Gideon's band taught as its moral: a few brave ones are better than many half-hearted. Under pressure of long and bitter warfare the tribesmen drew together in fierce clannish loyalty. They might quarrel among themselves, but each warrior's spear was quickly leveled against any outsider who injured or insulted one of the tribe. Thus, as among many such tribes, there were no kings, and the chiefs were only leaders of equals. Even very early they began to think of themselves as The People. To be one of The People was to have value as a warrior and a person, and so to have the rights of a freeman under tribal law.

Thus, as hunters and herdsmen, as raiders and conquerors, the Hebrews pushed slowly ahead, now victorious, now defeated, but always rising again in revolt. Gradually they mingled with the Canaanites, marrying and giving in marriage. They became slowly a new and mixed people, and began to combine the ways of city-dwellers with the old ways of shepherds. They learned the pleasures of buying and selling, and of the things that are bought and sold. They learned, often at the wrong end of the whip, something about slavery. Finally, around the year 1000, they were "civilized" enough to have a king, but they did not like the idea very well. Then too, Palestine was not a country where kings and cities could easily come to dominate as in the flat plains of Egypt and Mesopotamia. There were some small rich valleys, but they were isolated, and in between lay wild hill-country where only scattered villages could exist and a shepherd must sometimes fight a lion to save his flock.

During four more centuries the Hebrews struggled, never willing to adopt fully the new way, never able to cling wholly to the old. That struggle in itself represents, perhaps, nothing unique. The stout Egyptian tribesmen may also have struggled to preserve their freedom; in fact, about 2200 B. C. there was some kind of trouble, barely recorded in history, which may have been the last flare-up of their old tribal love of liberty. But certainly the Hebrew tribesmen struggled desperately, and (what is more important) the record of it was well preserved. It may still be read in that great book and fruitful source of religion—the Bible of the Jews, the Old Testament of the Christians.

That Bible of theirs was largely written down during the time of the long struggle between tribe and city, and in part it sprang from that very struggle. Unlike most ancient books it therefore preserved not only the idea of the slave-kingdom, but also the older ideas of village, tribe, and warrior-band. The great Jehovah was, indeed, Lord of Lords, but he did not wholly ignore the individuality even of a slave, and he had a marked sympathy for the rights of the small farmer, who once had been the warrior-tribesman.

As in a Great Charter for human rights, a story here and there stood out from the pages. One was of King David. Grown middle-aged and royal, no longer the ideal warrior who poured out the water at Bethlehem, he looked on the fair Bathsheba; to cover his lust he shamefully betrayed her warrior-husband into death. Then Nathan the prophet told to David the parable of the ewe-lamb, and cried boldly: "Thou art the man!" So David, even *King* David, could only say, "I have sinned against the Lord." And those are very strange words for a king, for they admit both that he can do wrong and that there is a Lord above the king!

Another story is how King Ahab took away the vineyard which was Naboth's inheritance. When Naboth did not agree, he was stoned to death. Then Elijah cried the vengeance of the Lord, with a curse so terrible that when Ahab heard those words, he tore his clothes and fasted, and lay in sackcloth *and went softly.*

Now, I say again, the importance of these stories is not merely that they happened, but that they were recorded in a book which came to be held sacred by many people. If someone should prove them both to be pure fiction, though I think that unlikely, their influence would have been just the same. How many a good priest have they nerved and armed in defense of the weak poor man against the great!

So that book preserved the record and hallowed it with sacred tradition: that the world had not always been a world of lords and peasants, of kings and subjects. Even if there were slaves, they too were not merely as dirt. And if there were kings, they like others sometimes cried, "I have sinned!" and went softly.

Of course the book was also in places a justification for slavery and polygamy, witch-hunting, the divine right of kings, and annihilation of your enemies by fire and sword. All that was not so important, because such matters drew plenty of support from many other sources and from common practice. The precious heritage was that the book spoke also here and there for a different social justice, and for the rights and high dignity of the individual. And since it existed, not as mere tradition, but as sacred writing, it passed on unchanged. Generation after generation, Nathan and Elijah cried out again, wherever there were freemen to hear.

Too many people think of the Hebrews as going down before Nebuchadnezzar, and after that, of there being merely Jews. But during centuries, while the Greeks (those victors of Marathon and Salamis) were tame cats in the lap of Rome, the Jews fought and died for liberty. They fought Antiochus under the Maccabees. They fought the Roman legions under the great Pompey, and stood a two-year siege at Jerusalem. They rose under Hezekiah the Galilean to fight Herod. They rose again under Judas, son of Hezekiah.

You can say "religious fanaticism," and shrug it off. I think it was more than that. They rose also as if to the old call of the free tribesmen, "To your tents, O Israel!"—against the oppression of the foreign tyrant, against their own rich men, the collaborators. They died bloodily in the battles; they starved in the sieges.

They rose again in the Great Rebellion, and their defense of Jerusalem became one of the wonders of history. After he had slaughtered and enslaved them by thousands, the Emperor Titus thought well enough of himself to erect a triumphal arch in the Forum.

And a generation later they rose again—in Cyprus and Cyrenaica and Egypt where they had been scattered. Finally in 132 A. D. they rose for the last time, and most dangerously. For then they fought not only for themselves, but as a spear-head of all the enemies of the Empire. The top-notch Roman general hurried all the way from Britain to stem the assault, and when he had finished, Judea lay desolate.

Yet all this is hardly worth my telling, except perhaps to show the importance of books. It failed, and so did not become a part of living tradition. Moreover, it was not recorded as part of the sacred writings, and so had little influence upon the more distant future. In later years, for a hundred who knew of Nathan and Elijah, perhaps only one knew of the continuing struggle for freedom, and even he probably thought it of little importance.

26

Some tribes from the north

In telling of the Hebrews I have reached forward so far as to mention the date, 132 A. D. To pick up the story of the Greeks, I must again go back to a time soon after 2000 B. C.

In their early history the Greeks were much like the Hebrews. They too came as wild raiders, and stayed as conquerors. They too came into a land of cities and more civilized peoples, which was also, like Palestine, a poor and hilly land where huge cities could not flourish as in Egypt and Mesopotamia. Like the Hebrews, they came in waves, tribe following tribe. And again, they mingled with the inhabitants of the land, and came to be really a new people. Finally, much as the Jews set themselves off from the gentiles, so the Greeks classed all others as "barbarians."

The Greeks emerged from that great northern reservoir of the Indo-Europeans. If no one knows much about the conquest of Canaan, even less is known for certain about the conquest of the land which was later known as Greece. With all the mass of Europe behind them, the

Greeks may have been more numerous than the Hebrews. They certainly seem to have made a more thorough job of conquest.

By 800 B. C. the era of invasion and conquest, and re-invasion and re-conquest, was about over, and the Greeks had established the ways of living which were especially their own. Like the Hebrews they kept many of their old tribal habits, but they took to city-life much more easily and quickly than the Hebrews did. In particular they developed their own type of city.

The usual city, as in Egypt and Mesopotamia, can be compared to a pyramid, or some adaptation of one. The Greek city, however, was more like two chunks of brick, one set on top of the other. The upper was the "citizens," that is, the freemen who were descended from the old tribal war-band; the lower was the peasants and slaves. Sometimes the situation might be compared to a brick with a half-brick laid on top of it; such a proportion would represent a rather healthy Greek city. If the upper block was very small in proportion, the situation was more oriental, and less typically Greek. If the upper block was about as large or even larger than the lower one, the situation was unhealthful.

All this was because the citizens concerned themselves traditionally with politics and war. Being descendants of warriors, they considered "work" to be beneath them. They expected to live, and very often actually were able to live, on the food, clothing, and other necessities produced by the peasants and slaves, or captured in war. Since the citizens might be as numerous as the slaves, they could not live in the luxury of oriental tyrants; in fact, they often approached the shabby genteel; still, they lived more or less as a leisure class, and were more or less equal among themselves.

This existence in the Greek city of a large and rather poverty-stricken lot of free citizens was of importance to my story. Not being wealthy, the citizens were often dissatisfied; they were therefore not like the priests and nobles of an oriental city, but had some interest in new things. Being numerous, they formed a larger population from which an occasional talented individual might emerge. Not having much regular work to do, they had to pass the time in various ways. Thus the Greek citizens were able to develop art, athletics, and philosophy.

The Greek city was probably in working order as early as 800 B. C., and the Homeric poems may have been put into shape not long after that time. In general, however, the Greeks did not begin to be very active mentally until after 600 B. C. From then on, during three centuries, was their great period. Near the middle of this time, however, occurred the famous war of the Greeks and Persians. So much has been said about the importance of this war that I cannot pass it over entirely, even though I, Man, do not think it as epoch-making in my story as do many who have treated the subject.

A great deal of nonsense has been written about the Greeks in general (perhaps as much as about the Hebrews), and about this Persian war, I think, in particular. It is still gravely said, "Greece saved civilization by defeating Persia."

To any intelligent Egyptian or Babylonian, of course, such a statement would only have been laughable. To him the battles at Marathon and Salamis and Plataea were squabbles between two warlike and half-barbarous tribes.

Egypt and Babylonia had invented civilization and maintained it for about two thousand years already, and were quite able to do so, thank you, without either Persia or Greece. I think that such a one would have been correct on the whole, although he missed a few details, not being able to see everything that would happen in the future.

And who were these Persians, that civilization could only be saved by their defeat? Actually they were another Indo-European tribe which had recently descended upon the city-world from the northeast, just as the Greeks had come from the northwest. They were almost as talented a people as the Greeks, and in many ways were more admirable. Justice and personal decency they had elevated into a religion. Their great king caused to be inscribed upon his tomb:

> *Right I loved and wrong I hated.*
> *I willed no injustice to widow and orphan—*
> *I punished the liar, rewarded the worker.*

The supreme misfortune of the Persians was, not to lose the war with the Greeks, but to let the Greeks write the history of it and pass it on down to later nations. All this worked out just about as if we knew about the dogs only from a history written by the cats.

So the Greeks won the war, and if they did not thereby "save civilization," they at least gained the chance to make it over. Did they?

First of all, I might consider whether the Greeks went ahead to gain for me any new important control over the world. In a practical sense, they certainly did not. They failed to invent any earth-shaking machine like the bow, or any new technique like agriculture. Except in navigation and warfare the Greeks indeed scarcely even equalled the older peoples.

In theoretical knowledge, however, the Greeks did better. Although I may be being fanciful, I like to connect this advance in theory with the typical citizens' habit of getting together in the market-place and talking. Before and after the Persian war, in the market-place at Athens and in a hundred others, the citizens talked and talked. Most of these billions of words must have been concerned with the common subjects—food and drink, sex, crops, weather, prices, war, politics, gossip, and scandal. As they talked, they sometimes gesticulated with their hands, and at other times they used their hands by drawing to illustrate the talk. There is a famous story that Archimedes the philosopher was drawing a diagram in the sand when a Roman soldier killed him. So, I imagine, a returned veteran, the scar of an arrow-wound still red on his cheek, might explain with diagrams how we licked the Persians at Mycale, or a market-place strategist might demonstrate the easy way to capture Syracuse.

But there is certainly some connection between language and thought. Just as a great deal of thought usually produces some language, so continual talking is likely to be associated with some thought here and there. In any Greek market-place, you could probably at times find a discussion in full blast about some matter not having to do with the passing present. It might be an argument about the theoretical and ideal city, or about some pure abstraction like space, or number, or cause, or motion, or even about thought itself. At its height the conversation of Greek citizens became the Socratic dialogue.

Through talk and through the drawing of diagrams which naturally went with it, the Greeks made some of their greatest contributions. Thus, obviously, they developed plane geometry, which was their foremost achievement in mathematics and in science generally. Thence they went on somewhat into solid and analytical geometry, and trigonometry. Also the field of physics in which they had most success was that of mechanics; here they worked out the laws of the inclined plane and the pulley, and these again involved problems in which the drawing of diagrams was helpful.

In problems which they approached by talk alone the Greeks did not get along so fruitfully, although even here they produced many brilliant and ingenious ideas. They talked about atoms, and elements, and evolution, and so we might think that the world never caught up with them until the time of Priestley, Lavoisier, and Darwin. Even more, we can quote Anaximenes that nothing needs to be held in position, and Leucippus that motion needs no cause, and Aristotle that there is no such entity as time—and these Greeks seem suddenly to be the contemporaries of Einstein.

But there is, I am afraid, a fallacy somewhere in this argument. It lies, I think, in the fact that their admirers make the Greek philosophers seem so brilliant and modern only by mentioning their occasional hits and by neglecting their many misses. Obviously, when a clever lot of people are speculating about all sorts of things, they will now and then make a correct guess. Thus, going through Aristotle page by page, you may be impressed with his idea of time, but you will also notice that he believed bees to carry stones as ballast in a high wind.

The great besetting weakness of the Greeks seems to have been that they tended to deal too much in mere speculation and words. They *talked* of elements and atoms, but many of them considered water to be an element, and none of them ever got round to breaking it down into atoms of hydrogen and oxygen. In fact they did not even discover hydrogen or oxygen.

Perhaps the failure was tied up with the Greek citizen's conception of work as being beneath him. Anyone fussing around with actual chemistry, not mere chemical theory, is certain to get his hands dirty. The Greek was interested in thinking about abstract chemistry. For the same reason probably the Greeks seldom put theory to work. Archimedes made a fabulous reputation by doing so occasionally. He was the exception, and even the famous Archimedes screw may really have been invented by the Egyptians. Throughout the breadth of the world, there is in use no important invention which can certainly be credited to the Greeks. Even when one of them came close to a world-revolution by making a little steam-engine, he let it remain only an amusing toy. After all, what was the use of mastering steam-power—there were slaves!

In discussing so many things, however, the Greeks

made an important contribution to my story—not in anything they discovered but by showing how to go about the matter of discovering knowledge in general. For, if anything can be talked about, it can obviously be thought about too. Moreover, if you get your opponent into a tight place in the argument, and he suddenly says, "Oh, there's no use discussing *that*—that is the work of the gods!" then he is obviously not playing fair. And, when he says such a thing, there is nothing left to talk about, and you might as well go home. Going home, however, was something which the Greek citizen apparently faced with horror, and adopted only as a last resort. So just for the sake of a good discussion, if for nothing else, you would be likely to leave the gods out of it. For this or other reasons the Greeks (some of them, that is) got into the habit of discussing matters on a wholly natural or reasonable basis.

A few of the Greeks really went the whole way in throwing off the bonds of tradition and superstition. The great physician Hippocrates declared that there was really no practical difference whether you called something the work of the gods or not. In either case, you had to try to find out what was causing it— "All things are alike in this, that they can be traced to preceding causes."

All this does not mean that the Greeks invented this natural or reasonable approach, although they may have been the first to be self-conscious about it. But the people who had made the great discoveries of the past must have approached life on a rational basis; otherwise you have to assume that magic and superstition really work. It also does not mean that the Greeks were not superstitious. Nearly all of them were—even sophisticated ones like Xenophon. In great affairs they consulted oracles. The Spartans missed the battle of Marathon because they dared not march until the moon was right, and some more dawdling for the moon had much to do with the crippling Athenian defeat before Syracuse. So about all we can claim is that a few of the Greeks, presumably like a few of various earlier tribes, were not superstitious, and believed in reasoning things out.

On the whole, the Greeks really accomplished nothing in gaining immediate control over the world, but by advancing mathematics and by re-asserting the rational approach they developed tools which others would put to good use later.

In the relationships between individuals the Greeks made no important contribution. They merely accepted slavery and conquest and the other basic ideas of the older peoples. After the Persian victory, Athens set out with really indecent haste to build an empire on the Persian plan—or, perhaps I should say, the Assyrian plan. The Athenians reduced many Greek cities to subjection, killed hundreds of free Greeks, and enslaved thousands of others. Under the mild Persian rule Melos and Skione might never have suffered the horrors which the stern Athenians inflicted upon them. (One of the greatest paradoxes of history is that the free citizenry who produced Socrates also condemned him to death.)

That basic Greek institution, the city-state, proved very soon to be so completely impractical that probably no one in the modern world would seriously advocate a return to it. Yet the best Greeks nailed the flag to that mast. They lived, and too often they died, in hopeless and pathetic loyalty to the ideal of the city-state. Even Aristotle, writing under the shadow of Alexander's empire, held to the dream of a tight little north-country city, although such a thing was by this time as much out of date as a hunters' camp.

The Greeks usually get some credit for propagating democracy. There was of course no real democracy in Greece. Even political theorists accepted slavery as part of the natural scheme of things. Still, within the rather large group of citizens, there was an ideal of freedom and equality. The Greeks at least invented the word, and developed the idea and ideal, even if not the fact, of democracy.

People often say that the Greeks contributed to the world the conception of the free individual. Looking at the whole picture, I rather think that the free citizen was merely the survival of the free tribesman, and as such was by no means uniquely Greek.

In developing a great art, the Greeks also gave expression to a great individualism. This whole matter of art, however, I find almost as embarrassing to discuss as that of religion. With such a practical implement as the bow, everyone will easily agree that one bow may be judged better than another according to whether it enables the bowman to shoot farther and harder, more accurately, more quickly, and so forth. With art, however, things are not so simple, and I cannot find any sure way to tell which art or which individual work of art is better than another.

A great many people have praised Greek sculpture, architecture, and literature as the finest in the world. But someone else merely has to arise and say that he prefers Gothic, or Chinese, or Aztecan art, and the lovers of Greek art can then only call him insulting names, without proving him wrong.

At least, many will say, "Greek art greatly exceeded everything before it." But this belief also rests chiefly upon the accident that until recently very little was known about the arts before Greece. Who, looking at the sculptured head of Queen Nefretete, or even at Aurignacian paintings, can say any longer that the Greeks were the first to master the esthetics of line and form and color? We know now that there was the Babylonian epic of Marduk, long before Homer. And a good thousand years before Alcaeus and Sappho, unknown Egyptians had already written *The Song of the Harp-Player* and the sadly beautiful "Death lies before me today."

Summing it up, I conclude that the Greeks neither made civilization, nor saved it, nor even re-made it very notably. They were, like some other peoples, a tribal folk who came into contact with the no-longer-creative king-and-slave civilization, enjoyed a brief flare-up, then were absorbed into the pattern of that civilization. They did not break the mold!

This is a true enough summation in one way, and yet in another way it is false, not because of what the Greeks did and failed to do, but because of the opinion which the later peoples had of the Greeks. Even if the Greeks were not very important in themselves, the fact that others have thought them important really makes them so.

What is the answer to the paradox? I should say that it is tied up with this—that there was one manual art which the Greek citizen did not feel beneath him. That was writing!

In this again the Greeks turn out to resemble the Hebrews. Although also influencing the later world through their sculpture and architecture, the Greeks achieved most greatly by passing their thoughts on through the written word. They did not make new inventions like the plow or wheel, or work out new institutions like kingship. But what they thought and talked about, they wrote down. Thus even the mistakes of the Greeks were important because they stimulated later men to think about the same questions, and perhaps to solve them.

These writings, a good part of them at least, had the luck to survive, and the knowledge of how to read them was never lost. On the other hand, the writings of the Egyptians and Babylonians were lost in the ruins of their cities and hidden even deeper beneath the mystery of scripts and languages which no one could any longer read. The even greater achievements of the villagers were also unknown until they were re-discovered through archeology.

So, for more than two thousand years, the Greeks held the field, with the Hebrews as their only rivals. The Greeks became the revered source of "profane" history; the Hebrews, of "sacred" history. Like the Bible, the

Greek writings included the trivial with the profound, the false with the true, and the superstitious with the rational. But again, the inclusion of the trivial, the false, and the superstitious was not important—for such things could be found in daily life. What was really momentous was that in the Greek writings the men of later centuries could find, along with much of the beautiful, noble bits of the profound, the true, and the rational.

Thus the lamp of the Greeks after a brief flare died down into the steady but dim light of the ancient way of life—the city of master and slave. The Greeks themselves became very docile provincials, and unlike the Hebrews they failed to put up a long fight for freedom. Like the Hebrews, however, they lived on for the future, gloriously, in their writings.

27

"Of Heaven or Hell I have no power to sing"

I, MAN, have never had a religion. There have been, beyond numbering, tribal rituals accepted by tradition, and individual creeds accepted by faith, but there has never been anything which could be called a religion of Man. Therefore I fittingly concern myself only with This World, not with the Other-world. Nevertheless, some religions have been of much importance as affecting the lives of my individuals and nations, and so they enter into my story, even within these limits.

This present place is the proper one for a chapter on religions. The period of the great Hebrew prophets began about 750 B. C., and from then on, in less than a thousand years, there developed all except one of the great religions which replaced the earlier ones, and which themselves have not even yet been replaced, although weakened here and there. Even Mohammedanism can be included by stretching the time by a few centuries more.

In general, as I look at the whole matter from a long way off, I should say that, first of all, these religions developed out of a certain kind of society, not the reverse.

Iron, to be sure, had grown much commoner, although the making of steel was still haphazard and uncertain. Some useful problems, such as how to supply a large city with reasonably clean water, had been solved. On the other hand, in certain details there had actually been a slipping back. Thus the Babylonians had made the extremely useful discovery of decimal notation, but with the decline of that people it failed to pass on to the Greeks and Romans.

For a long time, perhaps through all this period even, the people trembled on the edge of a gigantic discovery, without ever fully realizing its greatness. There is some evidence that in that still creative period before 2000 B. C. the Sumerians had discovered the power of running water, and had developed some kind of wheel by which a stream could be made to raise a small part of its water to a higher level. The discovery of the power-animals and slaves, however, must have worked against the use of water-power.

If it had ever been invented at all, the water-wheel failed to develop. Perhaps it lingered among backward peoples who had not discovered about slavery. Definite references to the use of water-power crop up in the century before the birth of Christ, but since the water-wheels then mentioned appear to be rather complicated and to have a kind of cog-wheel arrangement, I assume that they had a period of development behind them. At that time Antipater, a Greek poet of Salonica, wrote some verses which show that water-power was new, at least in his part of the world. There is something lovely and quaint in the way he combined his own mythology with such a thing, referring to Demeter the goddess of grain and the nymphs who were supposed to live in streams:

Demeter has told
The nymphs to do the work—
They rush to the top
Of the wheel,
And make the axle turn.

The first task of the water-wheel was doubtless the simple one of raising water for irrigation, but wherever there was enough fall to run a water-wheel efficiently, the water could usually be just as well run off at the higher level to start with. The water-wheel became more important when it was used to drive a mill for grinding grain, and it was such a mill of which Antipater wrote. About 375 A. D., a Roman poet gave a passing mention to water-driven grist-mills and saw-mills for cutting stone run by a tributary of the Moselle River. Since he made no fuss over them as wonders, I assume that such things were not too uncommon in his time. The innovation, however, began too late to make much difference in the Roman way of life; the ordinary student of the "classics" scarcely thinks of water-power as being used in the ancient world.

The water-wheel was by all odds the most important invention to come into my story in about three thousand years. But the world of the slave-cities was already stumbling and blundering toward its end. The astounding development of the new kind of power was to be left to the succeeding age.

The break-up of the Western Roman Empire in the fifth century has usually been taken to mark the end of an age, and I am ready to agree, although perhaps not for the ordinary reasons.

To people who talk of "the rise and fall of civilizations" the fall of Rome is certainly important, as the going-under of one of the most notable of them. As I look at my whole story, however, I fail to see that there has ever been a "fall" of "civilization," and I question whether the latter word should ever have an *s* at the end. I would not be too positive in the matter. Perhaps civilizations may have arisen independently in China, Mexico, and Peru. But I do not argue that point. In my story I am necessarily most concerned with civilization as it arose in that strip of territory running from Egypt to India. It apparently was by far the first to arise, and was always the most fully developed, and at this time of my writing it has enveloped and absorbed all the others.

Civilization as a whole has never been overthrown, or anywhere near it. Cities and tribes, nations and empires, have been conquered and more or less made over, to the great distress of their ruling classes and sometimes of their common people too. But the basic possessions of civilized peoples, such as agriculture, the domestication of animals, metal-working, and the traditions of living, have never been destroyed. As far as I can remember, they have not even been seriously threatened.

Even examples of the loss of individual details of civilization are not numerous. When something was lost from the knowledge of a people, it generally disappeared because something better, for the time, replaced it. A tribe passing from a wooded to a treeless country might learn to use brick for building, and then forget many of the tricks of wood-working. The Polynesians forgot the use of the bow or kept it only as a kind of plaything, presumably because their islands had no big game. In the same way, one religion sometimes yielded to another and vanished almost completely, because a second religion satisfied the people more fully.

So in spite of the fall of Rome, civilization remained well entrenched throughout four-fifths of its extent—all the way from Byzantium through the new Persian empire, into India, far off in China. It may even have been fairly well established in America. In the whole picture, the occupation of Western Europe by barbarian tribes could not, at the time, have seemed very important. The Byzantines may have worried, for Byzantium was almost a frontier town. But in Alexandria and Antioch the people must have passed it off lightly; those cities, although not at all old as cities went, had seen Rome come up, and now they saw Rome go down. In Ctesiphon no one probably gave the matter a second thought. In the cities of India and China, it was no better than a vague and gossipy rumor.

In one sense they were right in thinking the fall of Rome unimportant. It seemed the mere repetition of the pattern. Another set of barbarians had poured in upon some cities—just about as the Hebrews, Greeks, Persians, and many others, had done before. Any wise philosopher, shrugging his shoulders, might have said: "It is all the same. There will be troubles for a while, and barbarities. Then it will happen as it has always happened. Cities will arise again. There will be kings and priests and warriors, and on the other side peasants and slaves. That is the enduring pattern of things, and I see no reason to think it will be different this time."

Yet this time the pattern was not to repeat itself, and for that reason the fall of Rome was to mark an era. At last, after three thousand dull years, I can again find movement and action in my story.

30

Age of doubt

WRITING thus, as I am, about the middle of the twentieth century A. D., I necessarily see my story from that point of view. If I shall write my story again in the fortieth century, I shall doubtless have to tell it differently, not only because I shall have discovered more about it in the interval, but also because the existence of what *is* always changes the meaning of what *has been.* That statement sounds a little like Greek philosophy or Christian theology, but it is really simple enough, that is—at this time of writing, I find the European tradition dominating the world, and so I must pay the most attention to telling how that tradition developed; at some later time, if a Chinese tradition should be dominant, I would have to consider more fully how the Chinese developed from the beginning.

Nevertheless, I do not think it likely that the European achievement of the last thousand years will ever be made to look significant—not as long as I exist at all. As I look back, I see in my story only two great creative periods. The first began with the discoveries of agriculture and the domestication of the food-animals, and continued for some thousands of years through the period of the villages and onward until the city-civilization slowed down. My second great period of creative development began about 1000 A. D., and apparently is still continuing. I do not believe that I am merely dazzled because this last thousand years is the most recent and so shines brightest in my eyes. No, I soberly think after considerable reflection that this present period will stand comparison with that earlier one.

In the five centuries following the fall of Rome, I find little worth the telling. The tribes who had conquered Western Europe were fighting among themselves and were resisting invasions from the outside. Still wilder tribes were pressing in from the north and east: Northmen, Slavs, Avars, Hungarians. From the south the Arabs advanced. Until the barbarians and the Arabs had been repulsed, Europe could be nothing but a camp of warriors, and the modern world did not develop.

I say "until the Arabs had been repulsed" because of the way things worked out in the long run. Actually the Arabs were at the time a much more civilized people than the Europeans. I might compare them to the detonator, which does not make much disturbance by itself, but sets off the main explosion.

In the whole perspective of my story, the Arabs were originally another group of barbarian tribes. Like the Persians, they felt the inspiration of a religion which had grown out of tribal life and preached the tribal virtues, with the additional promise of a heaven rich in pleasures. Like the Hebrews, they came out of the southern reservoir of Semitic barbarians. Like the Hebrews and Greeks, but more indeed like the Greeks, they became victorious conquerors, overran many cities, mingled with older inhabitants, and rapidly absorbed the ways of civilization. Again there was that sudden flare-up which may occur when barbarians conquer cities. From Baghdad, through Damascus and Cairo, all the way to Cordoba in Spain, the Arabs fostered learning, made discoveries in mathematics and other sciences, and cultivated both the fine and the useful arts. From the eighth century on through the twelfth they led the Western world. Then that old devil, city-civilization, got them. They became conservative. They began to look upon the Koran as the final word, not only upon Heaven, but also upon science and society. Their collective mind thereupon shut up on itself like a frightened clam, and that was the end. Baghdad was no longer different from Babylon.

In their importance to the world the Arabs thus resembled both the Hebrews and the Greeks. Not one of the three managed to break up the old established system of kings, priests, and slaves, or to make much advance upon it. But all three joined together to pass a stimulus on to those who were destined to do better.

I can turn then to Western Europe of about the year 1000 A. D. It was a confused mixture of peoples speaking different Indo-European languages. These peoples had little previous achievement to their credit, and no one at the time would have considered them especially bright or talented. The best that could have been hoped for

them was that they would have a brief flare-up like the Arabs, and then settle down into city ways.

Indeed, throughout most of the history of Europe, any observer would have been justified in thinking that this was really in the process of happening. The descendants of the free tribesmen often sank into being peasants and serfs, and approached being slaves, while larger and more splendid cities arose under more powerful kings. Yet always, it never quite happened, and the ways of the ancient cities and empires failed to dominate.

This is very surprising. Why it worked out so?—that is the most important question to be answered in connection with the beginnings of the modern world, and I must give it consideration.

First of all, I do not think that there was anything essentially different in these Northern peoples. Were they more intelligent than other peoples? Because of their unique achievement any honest historian should consider that possibility, but I cannot say that I find any good evidence for it.

One cause, however, I take to be the different kind of country in which they lived. Western and Northern Europe was not like the Mediterranean lands. Being much wetter and colder and less sunny, it was not so good for grain, and was much better for grass. Perhaps it was not on the whole as healthful for men, but it was a much finer country for the better domestic animals. Thus in Egypt and Mesopotamia the pattern was always—large masses of men and fewer domestic animals. The typical animals there were goats, asses, and camels, which could get through the long dry summers by browsing on the poorest kind of herbage. In the lush pastures of England and France, however, cows and horses and sheep throve and grew fat, and from the meadows their masters easily cut enough hay to see them through the winters. In the numerous oak-forests swine lived happily on the acorns.

Thus in medieval Europe, animals were plentiful, and were cheaper than men. Scholars have been amused to point out that the ransom of the poet Chaucer was the same as the price of a war-horse. But they miss the real point. At that time Chaucer was a mere squire, and the remarkable fact is that such a person was held of equal value to a trained horse. Probably no Assyrian king would have considered a young warrior as worth ransoming at all, if he had been so unlucky as to be captured, whereas such a king might have paid a great deal for a good horse.

When people were scarce in comparison with food, mass-slavery could hardly exist. No medieval king could build a great pyramid; even if he could have collected the slaves, he could hardly have got the food to support them while they were working. Thus medieval Europe remained always a kind of frontier region, and kept the ways of tribal thought about people. A single warrior or even a single workman was always valuable. The individual was held in some respect, and therefore kept some self-respect.

There are other possible reasons. Perhaps a historian of diet may some time discover that when people keep more animals and eat more meat, they have more energy to make changes. Some scholars have attempted to connect the development of Europe with its more bracing climate, and point to evidence that when the Mediterranean lands first developed, the climate there was more changeable than it was in later times. Or again, I myself would suggest the very depth of ignorance to which people fell in Western Europe may, so to speak, have thrown civilization off its old track, and permitted something new to develop.

There is, however, another whole line of argument. Among every people there is always a certain amount of struggle between newness and tradition. One of the commonest sights is the quick dying down of the flame of youth, so that the young radical changes into the middle-aged conservative, except in a few cases. Yet without this adjustment any society might fly to pieces.

There is no doubt about it; most people want to live in a familiar world, not a strange one. Naturally, any world which is changing cannot be familiar, and to like a familiar world means really to like a stable one. In most ages the first reaction of people to anything new has been to dislike it, and to persecute anyone who advocated it. The instinct is sound enough, for there are probably more bad new ideas than good new ideas. The trouble is in objecting to the idea merely because it is new without trying to consider whether it is really good or bad.

If for any reason people cannot get rid of a new idea, they try to make it as harmless as possible by absorbing it into what already exists. They can do this when they have a large and strongly developed body of tradition and new ideas come at them here and there, and one by one.

The early Europeans, however, faced a much more

difficult task. Their own tradition was that of warrior-tribesmen. They might lord it over a conquered population, but they kept the memory of a democracy within the tribe. They hated cowardice and loved courage. They kept a dominating sense of personal loyalty to leader and band. Out of that tribal tradition came thousands of little ways of conduct so intimate that they can hardly be separated out as borrowed customs can be. Such, for instance, is the warrior-tradition, remaining strongly to this day—on the one hand, nerving individuals to fight in defense of their own freedom, and on the other leading them to rate courage above intellect, and to despise the arts as the resource of weaklings.

Battling with the native tradition, however, were three foreign ones. Christianity, preserved both through the Bible and through Church teaching, was one of them. Some parts of the Christian tradition strengthened the native tradition. Such, for instance, was the emphasis upon the value of each individual soul, which gave aid to the old tribal belief in the value of each individual fighting-man. Other Christian teachings the warriors could not accept and never did accept. The ordinary Frank or Saxon refused to take over the slave-psychology of turning the other cheek. He might admit that anyone taking the sword was likely to perish by the sword; but who wanted to die dishonorably in bed?

The second outside influence was that of the ancient city-civilizations. Looking about, the warrior of the Dark Ages saw the ruins of vast amphitheaters, valley-spanning aqueducts, and massive fortifications. Some of them he attributed to "giants," but more often he knew the name of Rome. He thus had always a high respect for the ancient world. As priests and scholars read more and more Greek and Latin books, the greatness of the ancient world in intellect and art came to seem as dominating as its ruined stone-work. Yet the magnificence of the Roman Empire was neither tribal nor Christian, but based on a pagan tradition of city-civilization.

Making matters even more complicated were the Arabs, who supplied the third outside influence. In theory the Christians hated and despised those dogs of Mohammedans. Actually, eager young scholars went to Cordoba, and sat humbly at the feet of the masters of learning in its university. They read that noble motto: "Four things alone support the world—the learning of the wise, the justice of the great, the prayers of the righteous, the valor of the brave." Or, at the other end of the Mediterranean, a captured Crusader found in Damascus a more beautiful and civilized city than London or Paris.

What then was the real way of life—tribal, Christian, pagan, or Mohammedan? With four teachers, all revered and all contradicting one another, the Europeans were spiritual nomads. They strove desperately to put the whole together. The greatest theological work of the Middle Ages was the *Summa* of Thomas Aquinas in which, to the official satisfaction of the Roman church, he harmonized Christianity and Greek philosophy. But no Aquinas ever harmonized Christian pacificism with tribal militarism, and explained why the Arabs (whose religion was presumably taking them straight to Hell) could nevertheless live so finely as scholars and gentlemen.

After 1200, with the decline of Mohammedan vigor, the situation was a little simpler. Europe had sucked the juice out of the Arab orange, and proceeded to throw away the squeezed skin. But three teachers were still left. The solution according to St. Thomas Aquinas might be official, but still there were protests, and before long there were Protestants. And, in the great majority of their daily acts, priests as well as lay-people followed the tribal ways of their fathers.

The conflict between the Christian and pagan ways was sharpest among the intellectuals, who were chiefly churchmen. As soon as they became scholars, they faced doubt. The medieval centuries have been called the Age of Faith, but that is only by contrast with modern times. Compared with the long period of ancient civilization, they formed the Age of Doubt. People who were sure of their faith, as the Egyptians and Babylonians probably were, would have had little to argue about. Those vast tomes of medieval theology are an evidence, not of faith, but of uncertainty.

In the late Middle Ages many a bishop and cardinal, after looking both ways, decided that the ancients had better answers for life than the Christians, and became more interested in Virgil than in Aquinas. Which one he preferred may not really have been of much importance. But the influence of both was of the greatest importance for him, and to my story, because he therefore kept a somewhat open mind, and might even look for new answers.

The conflict between tribal and Christian ways, however, was sharpest among the kings and nobles. The

Church taught of the seven deadly sins—pride, wrath, avarice, gluttony, sloth, envy, and lust. But a medieval hero like Richard Coeur de Lion was expected to be proud, and to give way to mighty rage as a gentleman should. He could not have held the respect of his retainers without being a huge eater and drinker, and an ardent lover of ladies. Of the seven, only avarice and sloth and envy were counted really disgraceful for a proper nobleman, no matter what any puling monk might say. Thus, more than in any ancient empire, the king and priest were out of step.

The conflict between tribal and ancient ways came closest home to the common people. They felt all the pain of the drift from tribal freedom toward serfdom and slavery.

In this enduring conflict of traditions, I find one of the chief clues to the refusal of the European peoples to follow the usual path of tribesmen becoming civilized. When there was no dominating tradition, people had to use their own minds to find guidance. When they had no authority to float on, then they must learn to swim. Thus the Europeans went on to gain new control over the world and to establish new ways of life for themselves.

31

It goes faster again

I, MAN, have often been called a lover of gadgets. There is usually some sneer in the words, and the inference that I should be more enthusiastic about poetry than about plows. Quite possibly—I put up no great defense of my career as a whole, and perhaps it would be just as well if I had never come down from the trees at all. Yet, granted that I did, I feel that something can be said for my love of gadgets. They have given me power over the world around me, and often I notice that the times which sprout most with new inventions also produce new ways of life for society and for my individuals.

After the year 1000 I entered into a period of new gadgets and new uses of old ones.

Most important, and earliest also, was the tremendous use of water-power. The record is far from clear, but water-mills, as I have said, although certainly known, apparently were not common in the ancient cities. Even during the Dark Ages, however, they were becoming more numerous. About 1080 William the Conqueror had the famous Doomsday Book compiled. It listed, incompletely, the property of England, a small and not highly developed country. The most startling fact for my story recorded in Doomsday Book is that within those narrow limits there were five thousand mills. Some of these may have been run by ox-power, but most of them are known to have been water-mills. In other words, even by 1080, nearly all English grain was being ground into flour by water-power.

Many readers have delighted in the colorful group of pilgrims in *The Canterbury Tales.* They have enjoyed the charming touch of the wart on the Miller's nose. But the remarkable fact about the Miller is not the wart, but his existence at all. The other professions represented among the pilgrims looked to the past, and their ancestry might be traced back for thousands of years—warrior, priest, merchant, carpenter, seaman, plowman. But the miller was something new, and in his use of mechanical power he looked to the future. When, in the *Reeve's Tale* the young clerk wanted to watch the grain being ground, and said he liked to see how the hopper waggled back and forth, he was probably the first character on record to enjoy watching modern machinery at work, and might be regarded as the ancestor of all those who since then have stopped, fascinated by power and rhythm, to look at a locomotive or bulldozer.

Windmills also may have been invented even in classical times, but they were later than water-mills in coming into much practical use. They appeared chiefly in flat countries, for grinding grain and also for pumping water. The uses to which water- and wind-power were put increased rather slowly, but the existence even of grist-mills alone was of incalculable value as pointing the way to future use of power. Also every poor little clattering water-wheel was an argument against slavery. Even if you paid the slave no wages, you still had to feed him, and so it was actually cheaper to grind by water-power and give the miller his toll.

This development of water-power is one of those unspectacular things that are easily passed over. Conventionally, gunpowder and printing are put down as the two great discoveries of the early modern times. There is no disputing their importance, either; but perhaps they have sometimes been held important for doubtful reasons.

Gunpowder, like iron, was at first specialized for use in war. Just as iron came to have peaceful uses, so gunpowder developed into high explosive and became valuable in peace also, but, unlike iron, it remained essentially warlike. Gunpowder, as used in firearms, I should compare to the bow-and-arrow. Again the prize went, not to force, but to skill. Some have therefore argued that gunpowder worked for democracy: "It made all men alike tall." I cannot agree, for the period of the development of firearms (let us say, from 1450 to 1650) was also the time when strong monarchies, approaching the ancient empires in ideals, were growing up everywhere in Europe. If the citizen had a gun, he might defy the warrior, but the citizen did *not* have a gun! In the old days, woodsman's ax and mower's scythe and hunter's bow were always dangerous potential weapons. But with powder and muskets manufactured in his own arsenals and held in the hands of paid soldiers, the king could laugh, and any revolt of either noble or burgher or peasant became much more difficult.

Gunpowder, however, really strengthened the cities as against the barbarians. As late as 1500 the Tartar horsemen were pressing along the Volga and threatening to flood westward across the European plain. But that was about the end. With the development of gunpowder the military power of the old-fashioned barbarians was broken.

As for printing, it was really a group of skills, involving the manufacture and use of type, the making of paper, and the perfection of printer's ink. After everything had been got together about 1450, the making and distribution of books developed almost as quickly as an explosion of gunpowder. The effects of printing were much the same as those of writing. Printing spread knowledge broadcast, and therefore tended to promote new discoveries in knowledge, for the more people who gain knowledge, the more chance there is for it to come into the possession of that rare gifted individual who can create something new. But printing, like writing, lent too much authority to what was recorded. "The book says so!" was still flung at the head of any inquirer after new things, and the words only gained power when printing lent a further air of finality to a text.

In early modern times came also much innovation in another field, of equal importance with gunpowder and printing. In navigation, mariners discovered the use of the compass; of even more importance, they mastered the practical art of sailing against the wind. In spite of

Phoenicians and Greeks, the peoples of the ancient world were essentially land-lubbers—"cock-crow sailors," keeping along shore, and steering, according to the slur, by the crowing of the cocks. They held it fairly advanced seamanship to make an open-sea run from Crete to Egypt or to stand across from Sicily to Spain.

But with people who faced the Atlantic, it was navigate the Atlantic or stay at home. They navigated, and built better ships, and sailed farther—the Northmen, the Flemings and English, the Hansa merchants, the Bretons, and Portuguese. Inside the Mediterranean the seamen learned also, and became better navigators than the ancients had been—the ship-masters of Venice and Genoa and Barcelona, and the corsairs from Algiers and Tunis. Perhaps the lateen-rigged boats of the Mediterranean taught the trick of sailing into the wind. With better ships and bolder seamen, voyages of discovery became practical, and by the sea-routes the way led on to the future.

It became the great age of discovery in space, and the three whose names stand out best as symbols are Columbus, Magellan, and Copernicus. All three were alive at the same time, and the dates of their discoveries fall well within a half-century.

Columbus voyaged to what the astounded people could only call a New World. He seemed to open up infinity. Then Magellan's voyage seemed again to declare that I, Man, had my limits upon a not too large ball, around which a little ship could sail in not too long a time. But Copernicus, who voyaged farthest though he stayed at home, came to see that this little ball was not the center, but only one of many and among the smaller.

Columbus, Magellan, Copernicus—in the short time since then, what have I done practically about their discoveries? As far as America is concerned, I have absorbed that to my whole. It is no longer a dream or a promise or a New World, but has become a pair of well mapped continents housing some nations. They may be a little better or a little worse than nations generally, but certainly not much different.

As for Magellan, I have scarcely yet begun to do anything about his discovery. My individuals are just beginning to think, not of communities and nations, but of one world. Yet Magellan may well stand as the symbol of the period which I am now entering.

As for Copernicus, I am yet only playing with his ideas in fantasy. The possibility of a voyage to another planet or even to the moon still seems as far off as a voyage around the world was to a Roman.

32

Some tribes break precedent

HAVING told how the Europeans got further control over the world and more knowledge of it between the times of Doomsday Book and of Copernicus, I must tell how they adjusted affairs among themselves as individuals during the same centuries and a little later. Here again, I think, the conflict of their traditions was important.

If I now pick up the story again about year 1000 A. D., and consider the ways of life, I find the Europeans living as warrior-tribesmen who had conquered a city-civilization. There were kings, nobles, freemen, serfs, and slaves; but the kings were far from having absolute power, and there were very few slaves. Nobles shaded into freemen and freemen into serfs, and the individual kept some sense of his own importance and liberty of action.

As civilization developed, population increased and cities grew up. Wealth, and the power which goes with wealth, concentrated in the cities, and kings and priests seized more and more power. As always, they gained support from that part of the tribal tradition which emphasized kingship and the loyalty of the tribesman to his chief. The rulers also gained support from many parts of the Old Testament and from nearly all the New Testament, and so they could throw the cloak of religion around their acts. Also they gained support from the ideals of the Roman Empire, which lay just behind them.

On the other hand, many forces opposed the growth of a slave-civilization. As among the Hebrews, much of the tradition of tribal life led nobles and freemen and even serfs to work against the king's power becoming absolute. If most of the Bible supported the kings, there were plenty of individual texts which could be quoted to the contrary. And behind the Roman Empire lay the Roman Republic. Abundant water-power and good pasturage and meager grain-fields worked against slavery. The new inventions and controls over the world were disturbing; the ancient cities had never had to adjust themselves to the impact of gunpowder, printing, and ocean-crossing commerce.

So, over the period of centuries, there was a struggle. The Europeans maintained a tradition of revolution. In the ancient cities, revolution of a kind had been common enough, but it had meant the mere substitution of one ruler for another. Most European revolutions were of this type also. Some of them, however, were definite revolts against the growing power of the kings, and leaders of such revolts might talk of their "rights" and "ancient liberties," by such catch-words meaning, I suppose, the greater freedom as individuals which they had enjoyed (or thought they had enjoyed) in earlier times. Sometimes the nobles revolted, as when the barons forced King John to sign the Magna Charta. Sometimes the merchants and artisans revolted, as when the Flemish or Lombard cities rose against their feudal lords. Sometimes the peasants revolted, as when under John Ball (a priest, as it happened) they captured London in 1381.

Along with this struggle the technique of representative government grew up, and this was the most important social development of a thousand years. It made practical in a city-civilization some form of government other than absolute rule. In a tribe or village it had always been possible to decide matters of common interest by calling the fathers together into a meeting. But if the tribe spread over a large area or the village developed into a city with dependent villages, there had been no practical way, in the ancient world, for these outlying people to leave their affairs and go to a meeting. For instance, toward the end of the Roman Republic most of the inhabitants of the Italian peninsula won Roman citizenship, but the practical power remained in the hands of the citizens who could vote in Rome. This permitted so much political corruption that before long any decent Italian would prefer to be ruled by an emperor rather than by the Roman mob.

But the Europeans developed the practice of having a chosen representative for each region. Then these representatives gathered together in a meeting or parliament. The system had many difficulties. The representatives might be chosen by a very small group, and they might be manipulated after they had gathered together. A parliament was often intimidated or bribed; its members might think only of their own interests, and betray the people they were supposed to represent. Still, half a loaf is better than no bread, and this halting experiment supplied a device by which individuals could act together in large countries without submitting themselves to the rule of a king or single city.

Yet, in spite of all the forces working against the development of a slave-civilization, things moved in that direction, as might have been expected from the example of all past history. After 1450 the "strong monarchies" developed, and the kings crushed the stubborn and long-continuing resistance of the nobles. The cities grew larger, and their masses of people were scarcely better off than slaves.

So it stands, if I look at the end of this period, and take France as my example. In 1700 France was the most developed country of Europe and the model which the others generally followed, even when they waged war against the French king. In many ways the difference between France of 1700 and an ancient empire was not very great. The peasants were no more considered than so many slaves, and lived as badly as many ancient slaves. The royal power was absolute, and Louis XIV could say "I am the state!" He had the support of religion, and so was declared to be king "by the grace of God," and "Defender of the Faith," and to rule "by Divine Right." Custom, crystallized into law, asserted "The King can do no wrong." Kings even took over the ancient custom of maintaining a harem, although it did not bear that name. Louis XV, however, approached open polygamy when he rode about with his wife and mistress in the same coach, so that the simple-minded peasants marveled at the "two queens."

What then should have happened by all the rules of history was that the development should have continued along these lines. If I had been writing this story in 1700 I would naturally have predicted that some empire would soon spread over Europe. This empire would have shown no great difference from the ancient empires, except that by the mastery of gunpowder it would have had insurance against barbarian attack.

Yet this did not happen, and actually the royal power was not nearly so strong as it seemed. The king with his "I am the state" was living in a fool's paradise. The explanation, I suppose, is that the kings were what they always had been, but the subjects were different. For as yet no one had solved the problems of the Age of Doubt. Tribal tradition, Christianity, and pagan ideals still clashed. Thinking men must try to harmonize them, and in so trying must think for themselves.

Thus, as had happened ten thousand years before, I came into a time when my individuals no longer depended upon tradition and explained the unusual in terms of the Other-world. Thus I moved again with breath-taking speed toward new controls over the outside world and toward new arrangements of living for my individuals. As in that other great time of change, the whirlwind was loosed; the stone was rolling down the hill; the demon was out of the bottle.

33

I learn about change

AT THIS point my story has passed the year 1700, and is entering upon the fully modern age. In many ways I am confused about this last period, naturally enough, because it is so close. Nevertheless, I am rather strongly convinced as to what is its dominating quality; as compared with all previous times, it is the era of change.

Change, of course, has always been at work, and without it I could write only a description, not a story. The Greeks, as usual, had an idea of change and one of their philosophers took as his principle: "Everything changes." But the Greeks, also as usual, let the matter pass as an interesting speculation; they did not really establish it or put it to work. Only in my modern period have I become really self-conscious about change. I have learned, first, that everything changes naturally—"Nothing is, but all is becoming." I have learned, second, that I myself can do much to control change, either speeding up or slowing down natural changes, or producing others which are not natural at all.

As a result my world has begun to hum along at a dizzying rate. The discoveries of the Neolithic and village periods were more basic and profound in their effects upon my life. But those innovations were spread over several thousand years, while the modern age has as yet lasted much less than one thousand. Its rate of change has therefore been much greater.

These modern changes have occurred in all three phases of my life: in my control of the outside world, in the relations of my individuals, and (although to a less extent) in my individuals. I shall take this present chapter to tell of the modern control of the outside world, because it became noticeable, as usual, a little earlier than the others.

First of all, even in my relation to the world (let me emphasize it again, even at the risk of an epigram)—"The basic change has been the grasping of the idea of change."

Nowhere has this been more important than in the connection with power. Change from one kind of power to another has always been essential in my world, but it was generally so slow and complicated that I did not grasp the significance. Thus, the power of the sun's heat stored up chemical power in the grass; the cattle ate the grass; I ate the cattle; then finally, on strength of that meat, I released the energy of the sun through my muscles. This was a natural change of power, and, I must say, a very roundabout and inefficient one. By yoking the ox to my plow I released the power of the sun to pull my plow. This was something of a short-cut, but still a long way round. The next step, and a tremendous one, was to use water- and wind-power. But even these did not produce a very profound change; they merely shifted the motion of the water or wind into the motion of the mill.

The real revolution in modern ideas of the change of power came with the steam-engine. I call it a revolution because it involved the direct change of heat into motion, a really earthquaking innovation. Some individuals were experimenting even a little before 1700. The idea became practical through the inventive skill of James Watt, my Englishman, and he obtained his first patent in 1769.

From then on, the idea of the power-change ran wild, as the uses to which it could be put became more and more numerous. By the discoveries in physical science I learned that not only heat, but much else was just a particular form of power. Among these were things which I had always taken for granted as existing in themselves, such as sound and light. By following down the alleyways, I learned about other kinds of power about which my ears and eyes had never told me. I not only learned about them, but I learned to control them for my own ends. Finally I began to learn that power in itself might be the basic fact of the whole universe, that power might equally be present, not only in things that obviously moved or burned, but in everything else as well, including the very structure of the atom itself.

Thus I had come to grasp a new basic idea. Granted any source of power, I might be able to shift it from one manifestation to another, for my own ends. So, if I want light for my eyes, I think nothing of setting up the series of transformations—from coal, to heat, to motion of engine and dynamo, to electricity, to incandescence of an electric bulb.

The second idea of change is basically the same as the

change of power, but in practice is still something separate. This is change of material.

Again, I had made a fumbling start in very ancient days. Cookery transformed tough and stringy meat into something which my teeth and jaws could handle. Much later, when I shaped a clay pot, it was yellow and soft; it came out of the fire, red and hard. Then I learned to change various kinds of earth and rock into copper or iron. But shortly afterwards the city-civilization ceased to be creative. The Greeks speculated about atoms and elements, but of course got no further than speculations in the direction either of science or of useful arts. After 1700, however, the Europeans took up the idea of change of materials about where it had been left three thousand years earlier.

That was the era of careful weighing and measuring, and before long I made the great discovery that many things which had been always thought simple and basic could be broken down into simpler parts. Thus water was separated into two gases, and common salt into gas and a solid. I thus came to realize that much could be broken down into a small number of what seemed to me basic materials. These I called elements. Eventually I even have begun to break down these elements.

But this was only the half of it. Having broken complicated things down into their simpler parts, I found that I could put the parts together again. Often this was very easy. I might spend much labor in breaking down water into hydrogen and oxygen, but if I held a lighted candle to a flask of the mixed gases, they went back into being water so enthusiastically that they were likely to blow me clear out of the laboratory.

Before long, I learned something more which was very surprising. By combining the simple elements I could produce certain complicated things more easily than I could grow or collect them in the old-fashioned ways, but also I could often produce something which had never, to my knowledge, existed before. Given some basic raw materials, I could go ahead on my own and change them into what I wanted. My ability was not unlimited, but it was considerable. Sometimes the end-product was exactly the same as that which I had previously grown or collected; again it was something which worked just as well, often better. Most startling was the transformation of my life by the production of materials which did not exist in the natural world or existed in such small quantities as to have escaped notice—such, for example, as chloroform, plastics, and the sulfa drugs.

Eventually my attitude toward materials became much like my attitude toward power. There is a famous story of a Greek; having discovered a principle of mechanics, he cried out: "Give me a long enough lever, and I can lift the earth!" So a modern might cry, "Give me anything, and I can make anything!" So far he cannot quite make good on this boast, but it is no more fanciful than the Greek's epigram. This idea of the change of material is the second of the basic modern ideas of change.

The third is the idea of the change in the stuff of life itself. As a philosophy, this is tied up with the doctrine of evolution—that the forms of animals and plants change with the generations. I have also become self-conscious about this kind of change.

From an early time I knew something about the breeding of domestic plants and animals. Again, however, I began to master the secrets of life only in very modern times, and I have as yet done very little along this line. I have not been able to produce new animals and plants as I have produced new drugs. Some of the old ones indeed have been considerably altered. Few people realize how much more efficient the modern cow and hen are in comparison with those of a hundred years ago. Even this slight ability at manipulation of life has given me much more control over the world. In the old days if a country was too dry or too cold to grow wheat, I merely used it to pasture sheep or reindeer. But now I set out to breed a wheat which will endure drought or long winters.

The fourth of the new ideas of change is that I, Man, am myself involved in change. Naturally I must discuss this matter, not in connection with control of the outside world, but along with social change. Nevertheless some of the change itself is tied up with the knowledge that I do not exist apart from the outside world but am linked with it. I can no longer talk of "man and nature," for I am part of nature. I need not think of "man under the control of natural forces," for I am myself a natural force. I am weaker than some natural forces; stronger than others. A river may rise in flood and devastate my cities; also I may raise levees to control the river, or restrain it with dams. But I should leave for the next chapters most of this story of the changes in which I, Man, am more personally involved.

34

"Take away the kings!"

IN THE last chapter I tried to tell about the modern control of the world in terms of four basic kinds of change. I did not even mention railroads, automobiles, airplanes, radio, air-conditioning, telephones, and all the other devices which one by one have given me this control. With my love of gadgets I, Man, am tremendously pleased with all such things, and I would gladly write a whole book about them. But this present book is already getting a little long.

So I shall leave out the airplanes and the rest. People know about them anyway. Everybody admits that they have made things over almost completely. An individual transferred from a city of 2000 B. C. to London or Paris of 1700 A. D. would have thought that people were living very much as he himself was used to living. An individual transferred from London or Paris of 1700 to a modern city would think people to be living with the aid of many fantastic machines. A modern person is not only willing to admit all this, but also is likely even to over-emphasize it. Then he will immediately add: "Of course, society and the individual's ways of thinking and feeling have not changed nearly so much."

This has been said so often that most people believe it, and I am even inclined to accept it myself. Yet I should point out that there is some kind of fallacy of thought involved. Just how does anyone make such a judgment on the basis of how much or how little? Just what change of social institutions or of individual ways of thought should anyone count as being the equivalent of the automobile or the airplane?

Moreover, while I am the first to grant the tremendous change in my control of the outside world, I also insist that since 1700 there has been a tremendous change in social and personal life. In 1700 the kings still had almost absolute power, and slavery or something close to it was in full sway nearly everywhere in the world. The father had close to complete power over the wife and children. People were hanged or flogged or pilloried for small offenses, and these offenses were thought to spring, not from the individual's heredity and environment, but from original sin or his own natural wickedness. These are only a few examples.

The basic change which has affected society since 1700 is the same as that which has affected my control of the world—the growth of the belief that "everything changes."

Today people believe that society changes, and that the change can be to some extent controlled. In 1700 this idea was not generally accepted. Most people thought that the world had been created at the ridiculously recent date of 4004 B. C. (I have already said how irritated this makes me—so let it pass.) Even if they did not accept that particular year, they did not think it very far wrong. In 1700, therefore, so-called "sacred history" ran back, although very vaguely, for 5704 years. "Profane history" did not reach beyond Herodotus, or only a little more than two thousand years. All history thus lay within the period of city-civilization, and even a philosopher could see in the past nothing but centuries of the turmoil of empires with the beginning as remarkable as the end. In fact, he was likely to think of Periclean Athens and Augustan Rome as the most flourishing periods.

In reality, so to speak, that philosopher of 1700 was standing at a slight elevation on gently rising ground and looking back across a broad and flat plain. Some low hills, which were ancient Greece, bounded his view. Beyond those hills the plain stretched on, and then gradually (out of his sight) rose into the massive and shining mountains of my great period.

But in 1700 no one knew anything about what lay beyond Greece, except as the Bible and the Greek historians and poets preserved a few traditions and legends. Therefore no one had much idea of the great changes which my own brain and hands had brought about. Instead, everyone thought that I, Man, had been created by God at a high level of intelligence and humanity. Since then (because of natural cussedness or through the Devil's prompting—the theology was difficult) I had had a constant tendency to slip down. There was the incident of the Garden of Eden, and there was the wickedness of the time of Noah's flood. You could point to the melancholy political theories of the prophets, Daniel particularly; or, for the future, you could shake your head over the magnificent but terrifying threats of the Apocalypse.

To commit an Irish bull, I might say: "People thought that things were not changing—in fact, they were getting worse." But even those who thought things were getting worse usually credited the worsening to the Devil and Original Sin, and did not think that anything of importance could be done about it. For instance, they quoted: "The poor always ye have with you"; doled out a penny; and let poverty remain as part of the scheme of things.

Hardly anyone asked the question, "Where is civilization going?" Obviously, it was not going anywhere. But even when there was a questioner, he scarcely went on to inquire, "What shall we do about it?" The answer was obviously, "Nothing!"—human nature being so unchangeable and depraved.

But now—after only two and a half centuries—the future of civilization is an everyday question, and even the comic-strips present the fantastical social customs of the twenty-fifth century. Every serious-thinking person admits the possibility, even the inevitability, of grave changes within a short period of years. Even the conservatives admit the imminence—otherwise, why would they be alarmed? The only difference between a progressive and a conservative is that the one wants to help change along, the other to retard it. Neither doubts change itself, and only a few believe that change can be prevented or that it is under the direct control of God or the Devil.

Thus in modern times I see the battle of the conservatives and the progressives. Both have some use in making the story more interesting. The conservatives prevent things from flying to pieces, and preserve tradition, without which I would soon be back to foraging or would disappear completely. These conservatives are those who possess a satisfactory mental state which they do not wish to see overthrown. This mental state may be based upon wealth, a job, a faith, or an illusion; it is important, no matter what its cause.

The progressives do not posses this mental state, and are a more complicated group. They include the merely restless young people who will later become conservative. They include all who are discontented for want of wealth, a job, a faith, or an illusion. They include the idealists who, themselves living the good life, wish others to share it. Finally, they include the powerful group of the liberal conservatives who favor moderate change to prevent greater change. The progressives are important as keeping the modern world from settling into the dull monotony of the ancient city-civilization.

You will ask why these modern centuries have the new attitude toward change. I can suggest many reasons, although this whole matter of cause and effect is something very troubling to me, and always has been. I would say again, as at an earlier period, "Change breeds change." The new control of the world also affects society. Remember also that the Europeans were spiritual nomads. Not knowing the answers, they thought for themselves, and learned to depend upon their own brains. Since I do not believe that magic works or that any god looks after such things, my opinion is that change is brought about chiefly by brain-power.

The new idea of the change of life-stuff itself was also important. When I realized that even species were changing, I could easily believe that institutions could do likewise.

Also important in these modern times (although few people yet realize their importance) were the new means by which men learned to study Man. The investigation of primitive peoples by anthropology has taught me much. Of even more importance has been archeology. Although people had often hunted in ruins for vases and statues, systematic digging began at Pompeii in 1763. That year is usually remembered for the Peace of Paris which ended the great Seven Years War and lost the French king his American empire. It should rather be remembered for the other reason. Since 1763, by archeology, I have doubled the actual period of history, and have some idea of my activities before the invention of writing clear back for a million years. This has completely changed my ideas about myself.

Next to the very idea of change, I should say that the second important modern change in society has been the establishment of the large democracies. They are something new in the world, and have come into existence against previous experience that, as villages grew into cities, democracy disappeared. As I have already pointed out, this usual trend was well under way by 1700 throughout Europe. Then something happened.

I am too close to the event to explain it at all clearly.

Democracy and the new modern control over the outside world grew up almost step by step together. Anyone would naturally assume that there must be some connection. Yet I really cannot point it out. Modern industry with its factories, machines, and assembly-line workers has often seemed on the point of establishing slavery under a new name. Perhaps it still may, but actually it has not, so far.

In 1700 England was most developed toward democracy, but in the following century she stood still, and the United States and France took the lead. Yet in 1800 democracy was down. It had been overthrown in France, and even in the United States there had been reaction away from it.

But there was toughness in democracy, and from 1800 onwards the story becomes a thriller. I would conceive Democracy as an imperiled maiden. The old villain Monarchy frequently assailed her. Slavery refused to leave off following her. Capitalism and Big Business—sinister but plausible fellows—insinuated themselves into her company. Imperialism got her drunk on power. Demagogy fooled her again and again. Monarchy even, exchanging crown for colored shirt, moved into her house as Dictatorship. Nor can it be argued that Democracy, like a proper heroine, always kept her virtue. No, she played the hussy with all of them. What is more, she has often been particularly odious for her hypocrisy, frequently bragging of her virtue when she least should. She has even lent her clothes around, so that there are always some masqueraders who are no more Democracy than I am Gorilla.

I am sorry that she is such a frowsy heroine. Yet she has great merits too. She means well, and like some other ladies of her kind, she has had perfectly amazing strength and vitality.

The sources of that strength and vitality have been many. But, to drop the figure of speech, I should say that people drew courage from the Old Testament, as when they quoted that trumpet-call: "Take away the kings!" They drew courage also from Christ's tenderness for the peasant and the slave. Patriots remembered Brutus and Cato. Forgetting that Athens existed on slavery, they read the orations of Demosthenes against King Philip. But, much more important, they gathered strength from their own tribal tradition—the never quite forgotten freedom of the Goth and Frank and Saxon. In America, the frontiersmen even returned to tribal life, and their influence was not the least in making the democracies grow stronger. Then too, as that old domination of the Other-world and the long tradition became weaker, men thought more for themselves, and most of those thinkers —being humbly born, like Rousseau and Paine—saw no good reason why some individuals should serve others, merely because of unfortunate birth. Finally, the democracies had the justification which springs from success. After 1800, all could see that the United States, although a far from perfect democracy, was growing stronger year by year. But the Russian Empire, though possessing equally great resources, seemed taken with palsy under its tyranny.

Let the record speak. In 1800 democracy was down to a flicker. Since then it has been up and down, but always farther up than down. At the present time I find the strange combination of cities and democracy stronger than ever, and giving signs of continued vigor.

Perhaps I should define democracy before leaving the subject. In comparison with the system of the slave-kingdom the contrast is so great that a precise definition is not necessary. By democracy I mean merely a system in which every individual counts for something. The idea of communism does not confuse me. Real communism is either (as I use the words) a form of democracy or a slave-kingdom with an abstraction—the state—acting as king. But, though I have tremendous respect for the power of abstractions, I know of no abstraction which has really been a king, and do not think it possible. Communism therefore will either be a form of democracy, or will be a false "communism" in which (just as in a false "democracy") some individual or small group has seized power.

The other great social changes are tied up with democracy. For a long time the most bitter criticism of the doubtful heroine was that under democracy the individual, while theoretically more happy, was actually worse off. "Freedom! Freedom to starve!" That was the only-too-true cry of the enemies, and they continued: "We take care of our slaves, but you let poverty and drudgery, and gin, destroy your workmen."

After two centuries of suffering, democracy at last began to put the house in order and to reply with the doctrine of joint responsibility. Its acceptance came very late, after 1932 in the United States; many individuals and even some countries have not yet accepted it.

It means, "While one eats, all shall eat; while one is clothed or housed, all shall be clothed and housed." Eventually, it means, "If one has the opportunity of happiness, so shall all." It differs from charity, which was the means by which people of a slave-civilization relieved a feeling of guilt. It is more like the tribal share-and-share-alike. It has sprung partly from fear of revolution. It has sprung more from humanitarianism, the feeling which developed when people sloughed off the ideas of the slave-kingdom and realized that individuals were not created as servant and master. Once anyone had admitted the common bond, he had difficulty in remaining comfortable in a world throughout which his fellow citizens were starving and suffering.

But once accepted, joint responsibility could not (except with disaster) be limited to doles of food and money. It led on inevitably to job-insurance, social security, public health, production for use, and all the difficult details of a planned economy.

Finally, as surely as I came down out of a tree, sooner or later it means some control over population.

This last brings me on to another idea of change. I have learned that like other things the people of a country are always changing, both in numbers and in other ways. Under the hurrying conditions of modern times, changes in population may also be rapid. Modern science and democratic government have tampered with natural forces chiefly by preventing individuals from dying, by fighting famine and plagues. This is an idea with which the individuals themselves generally co-operate enthusiastically. At the same time, the having of children has been determined, as before, by natural instinct, by custom, and by religion, because most individuals resent the interference of science and government in such a personal matter.

With the birth-rate remaining the same and the death-rate greatly decreased, the inevitable result was a rapid and ever more rapid increase in population. Thus the number of individuals in Puerto Rico, Java, parts of India, and other places soared until the situation has reached a kind of explosive point. For, as individuals multipled, they also had to increase the food-supply, and this often proved difficult. The result was a kind of futile cat-chasing-its-tail. The food-supply was built up by reclamation of swamps, by irrigation-works, by better agricultural methods—whereupon, in another generation, the population reached a new height. In some districts there came to be twice as many individuals as existed there a century earlier, but they were famine-threatened and living as poorly as ever.

Once more, joint responsibility becomes involved. Under the once-universal system, a king could welcome these new thousands of slaves for his taskmaster's whips, and if they at last starved miserably in a year of drought —that was only the will of the gods, and the king feasted merrily. Democracy does not approve of that solution. But if all mouths are to be fed, democracy must protect itself against too many mouths.

But also, a population has quality as well as numbers.

If the stuff of life itself is subject to change, democracy cannot wish to see it changing toward stupidity, docility, laziness, and the other qualities which make for slavery.

Just what the solution will be is still uncertain, although some beginnings have already been made. But again, the mere fact of the idea of change is of supreme importance. The stuff of my own life itself, I believe, is within my capacities to regulate and to mold!

35

Of my individuals still again

The modern centuries have brought tremendous change in my control of the world and in society, but no basic change in my individuals. They exist, as they have for a good many thousands of years, with about the same body and mind, possessing the same equipment of sense, the same repertoire of emotions, and probably the same reasoning powers. There may have been some little change here and there, but I would have a hard time saying just what.

The great palace of the modern world must thus be constructed out of the same old kind of bricks. They are essentially no stronger than they were in past centuries, and no more adaptable or beautiful.

Yet I would not argue this theoretical detail too hard. Even if the individual has not changed basically, everything around him has changed so much in two centuries that he too seems superficially to change. The possibilities of indulging his senses and of expressing his emotions have enormously increased. The modern individual, for instance, is probably no better equipped to taste sweets. Yet in early times, except by occasionally raiding a bee-tree, no one ever knew a really sweet taste. So much did some primitive peoples love sweetness that their women chewed the unsweetened cake to change some of the starch to sugar by the saliva, then spit it out and baked it for the rest of the tribe. Sugar only became common along with the control over the world gained in modern times, and it has brought an almost infinite new source of pleasure to the individual.

I can say the same for tobacco. If the question were put to the inhabitants of a country like the United States to make the choice between wheat and tobacco, I think that a majority might vote to eat barley, rice, and maize, and keep the pleasure of tobacco. And I would not say lightly that they were wrong. Consider also all the pleasure which has come into the last two centuries by the use of tea, chocolate, and coffee. In the motion-picture the modern world has developed what is probably the greatest artistic medium ever known—combining the powers of painting and music with the sweep of epic, the flexibility of narrative, and the suspense, immediacy, sensuous energy of drama.

In the close surroundings of the individual, also, have come changes which affect him so intimately that he almost thinks himself changed—in family relations, in child-training, in attitudes toward sex. At the same time, he has been largely freed from the domination of the idea of the Other-world; he is much less haunted by the paralyzing sense of sin.

Yet many have argued that the individual is the weak link of the modern world. They point out that all those pleasures, whether sugar or the motion-picture, are essentially only escapes making life bearable, although it is basically unbearable. This, I would say, has been the pessimist's view of life in all ages; if true now, it must have been true always.

Yet the modern individual is certainly under special strain. At every street-crossing, he looks both ways. If he is absent-minded and forgets, even once, he is likely to be maimed or killed. He is thus perhaps under greater continuous strain than the savage who may not know where his next meal is coming from and feels himself under some risk of being carried away by a tiger.

I also view with doubt the sharper distinction between work and play. In older times most pleasure was involved with serious occupation: parenthood, hunting, farming, and the crafts. Even festivals and orgies were part of serious religion, and art was involved with religion or use. But the modern individual spends certain hours in work, and then the whistle blows or the minute-hand touches twelve. Thereupon he becomes his own master, and is ready for play and pleasure. Under such conditions the individual is, during half his waking hours, still a slave. This seems to me an unhealthy state; yet perhaps I, Man, am an old fogy. As Apollo served Admetus, so the modern individual may combine slavery and freedom. It may be that I, along with the others, am merely looking at this matter too much from the point of view of the more simple past.

These danger-spots may show where the individual has not yet adjusted to modern conditions. Yet, when I see some boys cruising in their patched-up jalopy, they seem just as much in harmony with their world as any farmer-boy jogging down the lane on his pony, or any young savage creeping up on a quail with his throwing-stick. I doubt whether the strain of adjustment builds up from generation to generation. In his first few years the child comes to know his basic world; the changes which occur later may put him under strain; the earlier changes fail to concern him, except perhaps as they have affected his parents. Therefore the modern world should beware of the aged patriarch, for he is most of all the one who has lived through change, suffered strain, and gone out of adjustment to the world of the present. Now more than ever before, the generation between twenty-five and forty-five is wise in its own wisdom.

There are other arguments about the decline of the individual which I do not take too seriously. One is that under the reign of modern science and modern democracy he is losing individuality and sinking into the mass of the crowd. This is, I think, a superficial judgment, heard usually in the plaintive reminiscences of old people, and the petulant carpings of sophisticates.

In one way only I think it true. Looking at a crowd today, I see the individuals more alike in that fewer of them suffer from deformities and blemishes. Modern medicine, dentistry, and dietetics have been at work. Even within a generation I have seen a lessening of the numbers of those gross fat people who once achieved individuality, though at a price. Only the bald-headed still seem to resist suppression. Therefore, anyone reading the novels of Dickens or looking at Hogarth's pictures will think, rightly, that people varied more in those days.

Yet I doubt whether many would wish individuality to flourish by the multiplication of warts, wens, black teeth, goiters, withered arms, pot-bellies, and warped minds. Democracy, indeed, seems in the better sense to give the individual a freer chance for development than he ever had under the king-and-slave civilization. Absolute governments have always been notorious in demanding uniformity. Moreover, modern science as it concerns the individual seems to be working more and more toward the recognition of differences. It has learned that even from the same father and mother may spring two boys who differ basically in body and in mind. More and more, in education and occupation, the problem of aptitude takes the fore; the round peg and the square peg are granted their different holes.

As for the dignity of the individual, this is said to have declined through the discovery of my linkage with the animals. If I have no divine spark or any immortal soul, what am I (some ask) but a temporary combination of earth, air, and water? What dignity then can the individual possess? Yet these same questioners, I note, usually point to the ancient Greeks by way of contrast. And among peoples, the Greeks with their high sense of individual dignity had at the same time rather little sense of the divine-in-the-human and of glorious immortality.

As to whether I really have an immortal soul, that is beyond my subject-matter here, since there is no religion of Man. But if I ever had one, modern discoveries have certainly not caused me to lose it. The question of the individual's dignity must then be argued on other bases.

In my own opinion, as I have said before, modern discoveries seem to have made me greater, not less. They show me to be self-made—Man, the Achiever. I, not Prometheus or Oannes, am the hero of the tale. Already the story of pre-history is clear enough. The modern child may be truthfully taught that he springs from ancient and honorable ancestry. He can no longer be told that his race was created only a few thousand years ago, and since then has fallen into degeneracy through natural badness. Granting that he is what he is, the individual should attain more dignity by thinking, not that he is of a debauched race sprung from an originally noble one, but that he still maintains the traditions of a lowly but restlessly developing ape-man.

36

A summing-up, and some thoughts

In the beginning, I wrote that my story was as plain as an old-fashioned novel. Perhaps, as the reader has gone through it, chapter after chapter, he has thought it somewhat complicated. Let me now present it simply, in summary.

There are three periods. First, I foraged. Second, I foraged and hunted. Third, I relied chiefly on food which I produced by raising crops and keeping animals. (I have not as yet, quite obviously, got out of this third period.)

My ways of life have corresponded to my basic method of getting food. As a forager, I kept ways which were almost as much ape-like as man-like. As a hunter, I became man-like; I relied upon cookery, and made spears and bows; I developed the fighting spirit of the hunter, and the psychology of the wolf-pack. Many of these traits still remain with me.

As a food-producer, I have passed through three minor stages determined chiefly by changes in my manner of living in groups. First came the great creative period of the villages. Second, through a transitional time of decreasing change, I passed into the historical period of the king-and-slave civilization. Third, during only a few centuries, I have lived in the creative period of modern invention, marked by the establishment of the large democracies.

I tell here only of the forefront of my peoples. At every stage, certain tribes failed to make the change, so that even yet there are primitives who have not passed much away from the life of foragers.

This is all there is to it, then, as yet—three main stages, the last again divided into three.

Anyone has a right to ask, "What is your theory of history?" My first impulse is to say that I, Man, have none at all. But such a reply is nonsense. To write this book I have had to select some facts and discard others as unimportant, and facts can only be selected or discarded by being viewed in the light of a theory. Facts, which exist by billions, are quite unimportant in themselves. A fact is a homeless waif, until a theory takes it in and gives it shelter.

But at least I have no very precise theory of things. I do not, for instance, believe in that poetic idea of the cycles of civilization. If there are cycles, they must be in smaller matters. I see no tendency for my story as a whole to return upon itself. So, though I may compare it to a novel, I do not use the word *plot*, which implies a return to stability and an artistic ending.

My theory, I suppose is this. I, Man, produce history by making adjustments within a set framework. There are two parts to this framework. The first is the outside world of earth, sea, air, sun, and all the rest, controlled by what I sometimes call "natural laws." The second is the dead hand of the past which passes on to every generation a body, a mind, and some habits.

So far I have not been able to change fundamentally either part of the framework. The stars move in their courses, the earth spins, and the wind brings rain—for all of me. Also, I remain, and seem likely to remain, a somewhat altered fish, a slightly remodeled ape.

Let it be! Any game must be played by the rules of the game. But within the framework I make my changes, and the motive power is partly my clever body, but chiefly my ever-restless brain. This is pre-history and history—my brain working within its established limits to change the world, and thus to change also the relations between individuals, and the individuals themselves.

As to the question whether my story has any significance, I have two answers. To the universe, I imagine, it is of not the slightest significance whatever. (Of course, I must say, "I imagine," because I really know nothing about the matter for certain.) To me, however, I must say that my story is of supreme significance. It is all that I am and carries in it all that I ever shall be.

I prefer, however, to venture no moral conclusion. I would not say that my story "is good," or "is bad," but merely that it "is." So far I have gone, let me suggest, from *a* through *b*, *c*, and *d*, to *e*. Perhaps I shall continue through *f* and g, and even farther. But whether *e* is better than *a* I have no real way of knowing, except by applying some particular standard of judgment. Sometimes in this book I have obviously done so. "As a story-teller," I have implied, "I prefer this period to that because more is happening." But "good" and "bad" without special application are words which have been bothering me almost ever since I learned to talk—and that was a long time ago. I have not solved their problem, and until I do, I can give no final judgment.

37

I play at prophet

HAVING really finished my story, I now sit down to an easy chapter, and relax. The great trouble with prophets always, if I may be so bold as to say it, is that they take themselves too seriously. Their average of accuracy is so low that they had better think of it all as a game rather than as a profession. Obviously such a stupid fellow as I, Man, should not rush seriously into a field so ably cultivated by editorial writers, commentators, weather forecasters, armchair strategists, and all those authors of books containing in their titles the words *future* and *coming*. So I have headed my chapter merely *I play at prophet*.

I am not, I should also say, going to try any short-range prediction. Will there be a World War III within twenty years? Will democracy in the next generation be clogged by large numbers of old people preserved by improved public health? Such problems of the near future are not mine. A century is my least unit of thought, and I feel much more at home with a millennium.

This obviously is the place of anything needing to be said about atomic power, which is still chiefly a subject for prophecy. By coincidence, the manuscript of this book had originally just been finished, and was *en route* to the publisher when the first atomic bomb landed. The manuscript even then included several references to the subject, such as the almost incriminating sentence, "I am told that I am on the eve of grasping the secret of atomic power." Although I, Man, am glad thus to indicate that I was keeping abreast of current events, it is only honest to point out that no key-man of the Manhattan Project had blabbed to me in his cups and that by my standards "on the eve of" meant at any time within the next century or two.

Some would think that this whole book was thus automatically put out-of-date even before its publication. Actually, it has not seemed to need serious revision. Quite possibly, indeed, the year 1945, A. D., introduced the fourth major period of my story. More likely, it should be taken as reinforcing and confirming the importance of the great modern period, already represented as beginning about 1700, A. D. No one can really know at present, and any statement one way or the other is prophecy, not history.

First let me consider the question, "Am I going to continue for a while?"

I think that I am. There is of course the theoretical chance that a planetary collision will reduce me to ashes, or that a new virus emerging from tropical jungles will slay my individuals one by one until I too perish. Or I myself may unloose atomic power so that it spreads, like a fire by its own heat, until it consumes its maker. (This last would provide the writer's perfect artistic ending, and would certainly insure the world's going out with a bang and not with a whimper. On the other hand, one may doubt whether anything could be called artistic when there would be no one left to appreciate its artistry.)

Some are saying that I may destroy myself by war. War may indeed wipe out, or nearly wipe out, the inhabitants of a city or province; but no known war, even with the aid of pestilence and famine, has ever wiped out all the people engaged in it. World War II was, I suppose, the most destructive to life of any war; even so, the populations involved were so tremendous that the actual proportion of dead remained small. I see no likelihood of my actually destroying myself through war.

The two preceding paragraphs, including the past tense for World War II, were written before the dropping of the first atomic bomb, and I have not seen fit to revise them materially. Let us, however, imagine the worst war as yet possible—the world divided into two hostile forces, well matched, and hammering each other to pieces with atomic bombs. Even so, to destroy Man, bombs would have to be directed at all tiny hamlets in the great forests, at every desert oasis and oceanic atoll, at every Eskimo village along the edge of the polar ice. I think that all the individuals capable of making and launching atomic bombs would be destroyed first, and that wholesale destruction would then necessarily cease, leaving many of these outlying settlements still unharmed. I can assume my annihilation through war only by imagining some new Caligula, consciously desirous of ending the whole race. And that, though possibly magnificent, would scarcely be war.

Others have suggested that I may come to an end through the inability or unwillingness of my individuals to have children. Since certain countries have actually declined in population, apparently for this reason, I presume that the number of individuals even over the whole world thus growing smaller and smaller might eventually reach zero. On the other hand, people who do not have children do not perpetuate the tendency toward childlessness. All individuals are born of strains in which the ability to have children has never been lost. Therefore this particular kind of pinching-out tends constantly to correct itself. I do not think it an imminent problem, even in terms of thousands of years.

Eventually, it may be assumed, I shall disappear. But I have endured now for about 10,000 centuries, and see no reason to think my disappearance to be an imminent likelihood, even in terms of thousands of years.

There is a more common question among us prophets: "Is civilization going to continue?"

I think that it is. Although I can more easily imagine civilization destroyed than Man, still it seems to me a hardy growth. In spite of so much loose talk about its rises and falls, it has never been destroyed in the past. Undoubtedly there is a problem of definition. If by "a civilization" we mean merely something like the Assyrian or Roman empires with their associations of ideas, they have perished. But if (more reasonably, I think) we consider civilization to be the mass of such things as agriculture, metal-working, and social traditions—then civilization has never perished, and in fact no important part of it has ever apparently been lost.

Will war destroy civilization? Again, I think not—and for the same reason that I do not think it will destroy Man. Unless we assume the whole surface of the earth ignited, accidentally or suicidally, by one of the combatants, my individuals would presumably lose the complicated techniques of atomic warfare before they forgot how to build houses, raise crops, and keep animals. Thus the war would have to simmer down into an old-fashioned and less destructive one, and my story would move on again with civilization at a more simple but still far from primitive level.

My first and second prophecies may have seemed optimistic to some; my third will seem pessimistic to others. Because of the amazing developments of the last two centuries, many people assume that the methods of research and invention have been mastered once and for all, and that change will continue, perhaps more and more rapidly. I see no assurance of it. As far as anyone knows, the great period may already be at its climax and going into decline. Many scientists seem to think that they are on the point of transforming civilization by means of atomic power. But being "on the point" of something never assures its achievement. For twenty-five years a better electric-storage battery has been a prize to be sought by all the researches of modern chemistry and physics. Yet the storage battery has not improved basically.

Already some scientists begin to raise voices of doubt. Beyond their world of science, they say, seems to loom some world of chance. "There are," they declare, "certain matters about which we do not know anything, and *will never know anything.*" I, Man, am of course much too stupid to understand their fine arguments or to know whether they are right. But such statements suggest a loss of confidence and the end of an era. Perhaps already the period of slowing down is at hand.

Even in such a declining period, however, there will be great changes, just as there were in that other slowing-down period when the cities were developing. I look, for instance, not only toward more intricate and subtle machines, but also toward a renewal of domestication. The Egyptians had made a beginning with the baboon, but slavery intervened. Now, I should think, the baboon and the langur-monkey should be taken in hand, first for such obvious work as fruit-picking and window-cleaning, later (when they have been rendered more sanitary) for dish-washing. Before long, even the fishes of the sea may be herded like sheep, protected from their enemies, and driven toward good pastures. Eventually the fruit-trees may be pollenized by more efficient insects, and the soil made more fertile by especially bred bacteria and earthworms.

As to social changes—there have been so far only two social ideals which have existed along with civilization. One is the ancient king-and-slave pyramid; the other is modern democracy. History is with the first, and all against the modern upstart, but I am no great believer in history repeating itself. (At most, it repeats itself as a theme is repeated in music—with variations.) I do not think the problem solved as yet, one way or the other. There may be a struggle for some time, and which one will be victorious in a hundred or five hundred years, I'm sure I don't know. In the past the king-and-slave regime has taken over eventually for one basic reason. As population overtook food supply, the dilemma was always the same. Should all sink to a mere existence level, or should most people do that, and a few live better? The answer has always, and reasonably enough, been the latter. Democracy, however, proposes a third solution—that all should live well. But to effect this solution and to survive, democracy will have to quit her hussying, become a more careful housekeeper, and not be so ready to yield to the blandishments of any quick-tongued salesman who gets his foot into the doorway. Having accepted joint responsibility, democracy must also in hard-headed and unsentimental fashion set out to solve the problems of the number and quality of its people. Otherwise, the old dilemma will inevitably arise, and will probably be solved in the king-and-slave fashion.

You all doubtless wish to hear some guess about the future of war. With a king-and-slave regime, wars of conquest have always been part of civilization, and probably will be. Whether war also goes with democracy is less certain. A really democratic nation probably cannot make conquest profitable. The continued strength of democracy (of course, not democracy in name only) is not an assurance of peace, but seems the best hope for it.

Whether by growth of an empire or by some process of democracy, I prophesy with some confidence that within a century or two the whole world will be united under one government. The shrinking of the world through the development of the modern machines seems to make such a unification inevitable. If the unity is that of an empire based on slavery, that empire will from time to time fall apart, with wars, because of the revolts and clashes of factions. If the unity is democratic, that too may at times fall apart, with wars, as democracy relaxes its ideals or fails to put them into effect intelligently. But the tendency toward world unity will remain.

Before long, therefore, a condition will develop which has not existed since very early. There will be no backward tribes or nations. The present backward ones will either die out, or be absorbed into civilization, unless indeed some few of them are preserved in reservations. In that last case, however, they will be living as artificially as animals in a zoo, and after a few centuries will scarcely be considered even members of the human species.

But this is not all. In the past, my races apparently developed when the single stock was split and isolated into separate divisions. Ever since that isolation was broken down, the races have been mingling, slowly at first, more rapidly (like everything else) since 1800. As has been well said, when two races meet, they may fight, or one may enslave the other, or they may live as equals, but in any case they inter-breed. The race-problem, acute as it may be for the moment, is therefore a temporary one. For this reason, I have not thought it worth much attention in my story.

Only one possibility may prevent the race of the future from being a mingling of present races. If democracy, as seems likely, exerts an intelligent control upon population, some strains (although probably no whole race) may be found unfit. One may be too stupid; another may be even too brilliant, its occasional contribution of a genius not being held to balance its frequent contribution of maniacs.

And what of my individuals? If change dies down, they will be relieved of strain, and live more easily. But they themselves will still resist change. It is a long time since I was of necessity a hunter. Yet the thought of a spear-point well driven into the taut flesh below the rib-line, and the red rush that follows—all that is not always distasteful to me even yet, although perhaps it should be.

Very probably in 10,000 A. D. the individual will be much the same as he was in 10,000 B. C., although I grant that I do not know much more about the one than about the other. Yet I would not be altogether sure. I know now that the stuff of life itself is subject to change and that the change may be controlled. Perhaps some future period of civilization may concern itself chiefly with the change of the individual, just as past eras have been chiefly concerned with control of the outside world and with relations between individuals.

At present the individual is viewed as being pulled about by the two forces of heredity and environment. The heredity of future individuals will become the concern of a conscious control of population. The environment will be, as always, a chief concern of civilization as a whole.

The adjustment of the individual to his environment will be the special concern of a better-realized education. The individual of the future may well approach his education under the three great headings: first, the outside world in which I, Man, live and over which I always strain to achieve more power; second, the relationship between individuals; third, the individual himself. The first is science; the second comprises pre-history, history, and such related subjects as economics and politics; the third is a field which is not as yet even well laid out. It must include most of the so-called humanities, and much more—the adjustment of the individual to the world and society, his health and happiness, the means of his greater enjoyment of the world. Having gained in these general fields some basic knowledge and wisdom which he holds as a common bond with all his contemporaries, the individual may then more effectively go on with education to develop his own special powers.

As I began at the beginning, now I have come to the end. This is a little book in which I have told, in gossipy fashion, this and that about myself, trying to stick to what seemed more important. I have told more or less what occurred, and have sometimes tried to give causes. But this matter of cause and effect, as I have said so often before, always bothers me, and perhaps is just one of my illusions.

Other matters too still bother me. If I ask, "Has my career been good or bad?" I can only shake my head again about those two words, and weakly ask in return, "*Good* for *what*? *Bad* for *what*?"

So it is also, if you ask me whether I did all this of my own free will so that I may take credit or blame, if there is any. Perhaps free will is only another of my illusions, and all that I did was done by necessity as dictated by God, or Fate, or Some-power-outside-myself-which-may-or-may-not-work-for-righteousness. In this last matter, however, I have come to believe (being a common-sense person) that free will is at least the best everyday assumption.

Well, I set out not to take myself too seriously in this last chapter—and here I am in heroic posture, Man-the-Prophet-and-Poet, Man-Pondering-his-Destiny, Man-Questioning-Good-and-Evil. (Is my story most glorious, or is it something to make angels weep, if there are angels?)

Let me take a lower role, and be what I obviously am when writing a book—Man-the-Story-Teller. Then, to attempt a last epigram, I shall say—whether or not the story is good, at least it is a good story. The earth and the other creatures all seem to have changed little since I can remember. I have at least done things! Or, if you prefer, things have happened to me!

So I say, not only is it a good story, but it is the best story in the world. In something else also it differs from all other autobiographies. It is not only, reader, *my* story —it is *yours* also.

Index

People and places mentioned only for illustrative value are omitted, along with pervasive ideas like civilization *and* society.

Index of dates